Hindu Myths

Captivating Indian Myths and Legends from the Bhagavata Purana and Mahabharata

© Copyright 2021

All Rights Reserved. No part of this book may be reproduced in any form without permission in writing from the author. Reviewers may quote brief passages in reviews.

Disclaimer: No part of this publication may be reproduced or transmitted in any form or by any means, mechanical or electronic, including photocopying or recording, or by any information storage and retrieval system, or transmitted by email without permission in writing from the publisher.

While all attempts have been made to verify the information provided in this publication, neither the author nor the publisher assumes any responsibility for errors, omissions or contrary interpretations of the subject matter herein.

This book is for entertainment purposes only. The views expressed are those of the author alone, and should not be taken as expert instruction or commands. The reader is responsible for his or her own actions.

Adherence to all applicable laws and regulations, including international, federal, state and local laws governing professional licensing, business practices, advertising and all other aspects of doing business in the US, Canada, UK or any other jurisdiction is the sole responsibility of the purchaser or reader.

Neither the author nor the publisher assumes any responsibility or liability whatsoever on the behalf of the purchaser or reader of these materials. Any perceived slight of any individual or organization is purely unintentional.

Free Bonus from Captivating History (Available for a Limited time)

Hi History Lovers!

Now you have a chance to join our exclusive history list so you can get your first history ebook for free as well as discounts and a potential to get more history books for free! Simply visit the link below to join.

Captivatinghistory.com/ebook

Also, make sure to follow us on Facebook, Twitter and Youtube by searching for Captivating History.

Contents

INTRODUCTION 1
PART I: TALES FROM THE BHAGAVATA PURANA 5
PART II: TALES FROM THE MAHABHARATA 38
HERE'S ANOTHER BOOK BY MATT CLAYTON THAT YOU MIGHT LIKE 89
FREE BONUS FROM CAPTIVATING HISTORY (AVAILABLE FOR A LIMITED TIME) 90
BIBLIOGRAPHY 91

Introduction

The Hindu culture and beliefs reflected in the tales retold in this volume are thousands of years old. Many of these beliefs and practices were developed during the Vedic Period (c. 1500–c. 1000 BCE), so-called because it is at this time that the Vedas, a collection of important religious texts, were written down. Two important aspects of Vedic belief that repeatedly occur throughout this book have to do with the concept of Dharma on the one hand and the Vedic caste system on the other.

Dharma is a concept common to Hinduism, Buddhism, and several other Asian religions. It is a complex idea that describes and encapsulates the order of the universe and is seen as a kind of overarching law that human beings must follow for life to be both orderly and, on a grand scale, even possible. According to Hindu belief, under the umbrella of Dharma are laws, religious practices, and social structures that all human beings are required to adhere to. Violation of Dharma is seen as a severe transgression that carries with it equally severe penalties.

The Vedic caste system was broken into four categories: Brahmin, Kshatriya, Vaishya, and Shudra. The Brahmins were the religious caste and held the highest position. Below but nearly coequal with the Brahmins were the Kshatriyas, the warriors, who often held political power. Vaishyas were agriculturalists and tradespeople. The lowest caste was that of the Shudras, who were laborers and artisans. Unlike members of the other three castes, Shudras were not allowed to become literate or learn the Vedas.

The Hindu pantheon is richly peopled with many different gods, goddesses, and lesser but still divine (or infernal) beings characterized by features such as multiple heads or limbs or special skin coloring—many deities have skin either partly or entirely blue. In Vedic times, the two most important deities were the twin brothers Indra, the god of storms and war, and Agni, the god of fire. These two gods were replaced after the end of the Vedic Period by the *Trimurti*, the three gods Brahma, Vishnu, and Shiva, who together are the most important and powerful deities in the Hindu pantheon.

In addition to these greater deities are several lesser beings, such as Nagas (half-serpent, half-human beings), Yakshas (nature spirits connected to forests and other wild places), and Rakshasas (evil supernatural beings with a taste for human flesh). Divine beings are also categorized as Devas, or good beings, or Ashuras. They are usually considered to be evil—although as you will see in the stories of the battle between Indra and the demon Vritrasura in the *Bhagavata Purana* and the Ashura Maya's construction of a palace for Prince Yudhisthira in the *Mahabharata*, the line between good and evil often can be deliberately and richly blurred.

The *Bhagavata Purana* and *Mahabharata* are the sources for the tales in this current volume. Both are post-Vedic texts and contain important and lively Hindu myths and legends about gods, demons, and heroes. According to tradition and statements within each of these texts, the person who first wrote them was the Hindu sage Krishna Dvaipayana, a pseudohistorical figure also known by the title *Vyasa*, which means "compiler" in Sanskrit.

The *Bhagavata Purana* is one of the so-called *Mahapuranas* or greater Purana texts, which are collections of Sanskrit writings containing myths and works of philosophy, theology, cosmology, and other topics. The *Bhagavata Purana* was probably compiled between the eighth and tenth centuries CE. This *Purana* is particularly focused on the god Krishna and is an important text for devotees to Vishnu. Among the stories in the *Bhagavata Purana* retold here are the tales of the battle between Indra and Vritrasura, a reworked and expanded telling of the conflict between those two beings that is repeatedly referenced in the ancient hymns of the *Rig Veda*; the story of prince Yayati and his bride Devayani; the conflict between Daksha and his son-in-law, the god Shiva; and Krishna's defeat of the serpent-king Kaliya.

The *Mahabharata* is one of the world's great epics, following the exploits and defeats of the princes of the Kuru Kingdom. At the heart of this epic is the feud between the Pandavas and Kauravas, two sets of royal cousins who eventually meet in an apocalyptic battle to determine who has the right to the throne of Hastinapura, the capital of the Kuru Kingdom. Hastinapura still exists today; it is a city in north-central India that lies west of the Ganges in the plain south of the Himalayas in Uttar Pradesh. The *Mahabharata* may be based on historical events dating to the ninth and eighth centuries BCE, but the bulk of the text was compiled several hundred years later.

The *Mahabharata* is the longest epic poem in the world; it is ten times as long as Homer's *Iliad* and *Odyssey* combined and four times as long as the *Ramayana*, India's other major epic text. In addition to the plot and action of the story, the *Mahabharata* also contains philosophical and theological excurses. One of the most important and famous of these is the "Bhagavad Gita," a section of the *Mahabharata* wherein the hero Arjuna and his best friend, the god Krishna, debate together philosophy and ethics, Dharma, whether any war may be called "just," and the rightness or wrongness of armed conflict against one's kin.

The tales from the *Mahabharata* retold here include the story of King Shantanu, which is the story that opens the epic as a whole, and the tale of Shantanu's son Devavrata, who earns the epithet

"Bhishma" ("terrible" in Sanskrit) when he takes a solemn oath to renounce his throne and remain celibate for the rest of his life. In the story of the burning of the Khandava Forest, you will see the friendship between Krishna and Arjuna and their martial prowess as they battle Indra and many other gods in order that the fire-god Agni might consume the forest. In this story, the seed of the feud between the Pandavas and Kauravas is created and planted. The book ends with a more lighthearted tale of the hero Bhima's encounter with his half-brother, the monkey-god Hanuman, which happens while Bhima is on a mission to find some special flowers for his wife.

All of the stories presented are but a minute taste of the richness of Hindu myth and legend. However, perhaps most importantly, these tales are more than just legends of heroic or divine exploits; they are also repositories for complex and sophisticated philosophical arguments about the social and cosmic orders, choice and fate, good and evil, and the primordial processes of death, birth, and rebirth.

Part I: Tales from the Bhagavata Purana

Indra and Vritrasura

The tale of the combat between Indra and Vritrasura retold below is found in the Bhagavata Purana. Here, the storm god Indra commits the mortal sin of killing his guru, Viswarupa, whose father then summons the great demon Vritrasura and tasks him with avenging the death of his son. But Vritrasura turns out to be a much more complex being than his initial rapacity might indicate; during his final battle with Indra, he engages in a philosophical soliloquy about life and death and the benefits of devotion to the god Vishnu.

The aswamedha yagna, the ritual that purges Indra of the sin of having killed VitrAshura, was an ancient rite meant to ensure the legitimacy of a new king's rule. In this rite, one of the king's horses was chosen to run free for a year. A company of warriors went along with the horse. Anyone who could slay the warriors and take the horse got the right to become king, but if the year passed without the horse being captured, it was brought back to the king's capital and sacrificed. The legitimacy of Indra's rule, and the absolution of his sin, is thus assured through the performance of this rite.

There came a time when the great Indra was king over the three worlds and gloried in his power. He sat upon his jeweled throne with his wife Sachi by his side, and all of Indra's court praised him. Musicians played upon their instruments, and singers sang of his prowess while beautiful apsaras danced. All of the divine beings who served Indra—the Maruts, the Rudras, the Adityas, and many others—gathered there to pledge their loyalty to Indra and praise him.

In the middle of this celebration, the great sage Brihaspati came into the throne room. Brihaspati was the guru of all the Devas, the divine beings who do good in the world, and he especially was the guru of Indra himself. Indra saw Brihaspati enter the room, but he was so immersed in his pride that he did not rise from his seat, nor did he greet Brihaspati or do him any other honor as he ought to have done. Brihaspati said nothing about this insult but rather turned around and left Indra's court without a word.

No sooner had the door closed behind the great guru than Indra leaped out of his seat and cried, "Alas for my great arrogance! I have insulted my teacher, who only ever helped me learn to do good!"

Indra ran out of the throne room, thinking to catch up to Brihaspati and beg forgiveness, but it was as if the sage had vanished into thin air. Indra looked in every place he could think of, but he could not find Brihaspati. He sent messengers throughout the whole world to seek the guru, but all of them returned without having learned anything about where Brihaspati had gone.

"What shall I do?" Indra cried. "How shall I rule my kingdom without my guru's wisdom to guide me? Alas that my pride was more important than my humility!"

It didn't take long before the Ashuras learned that Brihaspati had abandoned Indra and the Devas.

"Go and attack them now," Sukra said, the guru of the Ashuras. "They are helpless and will not be able to withstand you."

The Ashuras heeded the words of their guru and attacked the Devas. The Devas fought valiantly, but they were quickly overcome. They ran to Brahma, chastised by their defeat and wounded with many wounds.

Brahma said, "You have learned the value of a guru's wisdom. You have been abandoned by your guru, and this has weakened you. The Ashuras know this well, for once they insulted their guru and suffered defeat because of it."

"Lord Brahma, what must we do?" Indra asked.

"Go to Rishi Viswarupa, son of the craftsman Tvashtar," Brahma replied. "Viswarupa is very wise and will likely agree to become your guru if you treat him respectfully."

Indra and the Devas went to Viswarupa.

They knelt before him and said, "Wise Viswarupa, we are your elders, but even so, we have come to ask your help. We had a battle with the evil Ashuras, and they defeated us because we have no guru of our own. Remember that it is the duty of the younger to serve their elders. The son must serve the father, and the nephew the uncle. Remember that Lord Vishnu lives within all creatures, who are reflections of him. We beg of you, be our guru and our priest, and perform the holy ceremonies on our behalf!"

"It is not good for a guru to also be a priest, but likewise it is not good to refuse to help one who is in distress. I will be your guru and perform the holy ceremonies for you," Viswarupa replied.

And so it was that Viswarupa became the guru and priest for the Devas. He performed all the holy ceremonies they wanted and always performed them well and completely. He even used his powers to take treasure from the Ashuras and give it to the Devas, and even Guru Sukra was unable to stop him. Viswarupa taught Indra how to don the spiritual armor of Lord Vishnu, and when Indra had learned all that Viswarupa had to teach about this, he led the Devas into battle against the Ashuras. This time, the Devas put the Ashuras to rout, for when Indra and the Devas were clad in that holy armor, none could withstand them.

Now, although Viswarupa performed holy ceremonies and made sacrifices on behalf of the Devas, he always gave a portion of that sacrifice to the Ashuras because his mother was an Ashura. Brahma had warned Indra about this, and one day Indra caught Viswarupa giving part of the offering to the Ashuras. Indra became so furious that he took his sword and lopped off each of Viswarupa's three heads. The first head was the one that Viswarupa used to drink the holy soma drink; this head became the kapinjala bird. The second head was the one that Viswarupa used to drink wine, and it became the kalvinka bird. The third head Viswarupa used to eat food, and it became the tittiri.

Indra acknowledged that he had committed a grave sin by killing a Brahmin. He, therefore, did hard penance for a whole year in expiation, but even at the end of the year, he knew his sin still lingered upon him.

"I cannot bear this penance any longer. I must ask others to take it from me," Indra said.

Indra gave a fourth portion of his penance to the earth, saying that in return, any pits or clefts in the earth would be refilled. Indra's penance became manifest on the earth as the places where no living things can grow.

Indra gave the trees a fourth portion of his penance, saying that in return, any branches that are lopped off will be able to regrow. Indra's penance became manifest in the trees in their oozing of sap and resin from places where they are wounded.

Indra gave the women a fourth portion of his penance, saying that in return, they would still feel desire even when they were pregnant. Indra's penance became manifest in the women in their monthly periods.

Indra gave the waters a fourth portion of his penance, saying that in return, anything that was mixed with water would increase its substance. Indra's penance became manifest in the waters as foam and bubbles. Anyone who removes froth or bubbles from water is removing sin from them.

Viswarupa was the son of the craftsman Tvashtar, the one who made Indra's mighty mace. When Tvashtar heard that Indra had slain his son, he became enraged. He summoned a great Ashura and commanded it to slay Indra. However, it was not yet ready to attack Indra on the day that it was summoned, so Tvashtar kept it for a time in his abode. Every day, the Ashura grew and became more fearsome until finally, he was so gigantic that the earth shook every time he took a step, and his huge, tusked mouth was big enough to swallow an entire mountain at one gulp. Every creature that saw this Ashura ran from it in terror, but Tvashtar called it his son and named it Vritrasura.

Indra and the Devas saw Vritrasura and were horrified. They attacked the monster with every divine weapon they had, but nothing had any effect. Even worse, every time they threw a weapon at Vritrasura, he would open his mouth and swallow it, and with every weapon he swallowed, he became more powerful. Seeing that they could not overcome the great beast, the Devas fled to the dwelling of Lord Vishnu to beg his aid.

Indra cried, "Lord Vishnu, holy one! Save us from this great Ashura, this demon who is greater even than Yama, the god of death himself! Even Yama has been put to flight by this Vritrasura. We beg you, save us!"

Vishnu heard the prayers of the Devas and blessed them by appearing before them. He appeared in the company of sixteen servants, all of whom had blue skin and four arms like their beloved lord. The Devas fell down in worship, giving all praise to Lord Vishnu, and were overcome by the joy of being in his presence.

Finally, Indra said, "Great Lord Vishnu, you know that we have come here to ask for your aid in killing the monster Vritrasura. That beast has swallowed every one of our divine weapons, and with each one he devoured, he became more powerful. If we do not slay him soon, he surely will devour everything in his path, and the three worlds will be no more."

Vishnu replied, "Your hymn is very beautiful and warms my heart. I give you thanks. And now I will tell you what to do. Go to the Rishi Dadichi. Tell him that he must give his body to the Ashvin twins who are here with you today." Then Vishnu said to the Ashvins, "You must be the ones to ask Dadichi for his body. He will not refuse you. When he is dead, take his bones, which are made of adamant, to the god Viswakarman, the great craftsman and architect. Ask Viswakarman to make a weapon for Indra, the great thunderbolt that is the only thing that can kill Vritrasura. When Vritrasura dies, you Devas will get back all your divine weapons."

Then Vishnu gave the Devas his blessing and vanished.

Indra and the Devas went to the ashram of Rishi Dadichi.

The Rishi already knew through his wisdom why the Devas had come. "It is an odd thing for immortal beings to ask one as mortal as I to give up his life. Death is a painful thing for us and not endured willingly, even should Lord Vishnu himself ask it of us."

The Devas replied, "We know that this is a very great thing we ask of you, a great and difficult thing. We wish we could do otherwise, but the very existence of the universe depends on your sacrifice."

"Does not the Dharma teach us that it is our duty to give joy to all beings? Yes, I will give you my body."

Rishi then sat down and stilled his mind. He put all his thought onto the Brahman, and after a moment, his life departed.

Indra took the bones from the Rishi's body and gave them to Viswakarman. Viswakarman fashioned them into a mighty mace, a thunderbolt that he named Vajra.

Indra took the mace from Viswakarman and mounted his war elephant, Airavata. Indra led the army of the Devas against Vritrasura and his army. Vritrasura's army was fearsome to behold, being composed of all manner of demons and foul creatures, but the Devas did not quail. The evil Ashuras faced the army of the Devas, and then suddenly they attacked, sending up a war cry that shook the heavens. The Ashuras flung every weapon imaginable at the Devas, but not one found its mark. The Devas fought calmly and skillfully, destroying every divine weapon the Ashuras hurled at them.

When the Ashuras ran out of weapons, they uprooted mountains and cast those at the Devas, but even the mountains had no effect. The Devas parried them easily, breaking them into pieces, none of which touched a single Deva. The Devas were able to face these onslaughts with grace and skill because Lord Vishnu had given them his blessing. The Ashuras saw that nothing they could throw at the Devas would harm them, and they became afraid.

They turned to run away, but when Vritrasura saw his army fleeing, he roared at them. "Why do you run, you cowards? Death will find you sooner or later, no matter where you go. Why not die nobly, in battle? That is one of the best deaths, but you will not find it if you run from it!"

Even the roars of Vritrasura could not stem the rout. The Ashuras were in such terror of the army of light that they kept running, even as Vritrasura cursed them.

Vritrasura then roared at the Devas. "Shooting a fleeing enemy in the back is cowardice! Why waste your divine weapons on a pack of worthless fools? If you want battle, battle you shall have, and you shall have it with me!"

So fearsome was Vritrasura that the Devas all fell unconscious before his fury, all but the brave Indra. Indra took his mace and hurled it with all his might at the great beast. Vritrasura only laughed, catching the weapon as easily as he might a child's ball. Then Vritrasura aimed a great blow at the face of Indra's brave war elephant. The mace landed hard, making blood flow copiously from Airavata's mouth. The elephant staggered back, moaning in pain and eager to escape his enemy. Indra spoke comfortingly to his companion and then laid his hands upon the wound, healing it instantly. His pain gone, Airavata regained his courage and once again stood stoutly against the foe.

Vritrasura saw Indra astride the fierce Airavata and said quietly, "It is good that we should face one another in battle, and it will be better when this battle ends in victory for me. You slew my brother, your guru, which is against everything that is right, and you slew him knowing this. He trusted you, and you beheaded him.

"Go ahead and fling your Vajra at me. I am not afraid of it, just as I was not afraid of your mace. If you do manage to kill me, I will simply lay aside this mortal body, and there is no shame in that since I will go on to eternal glory in heaven. And this is what I wish for above all else, to be in heaven, seated at the feet of Lord Vishnu, who calls me to himself, a joy and a privilege that no amount of wealth can buy."

Indra was astonished to hear such words from the mouth of a foul Ashura, but he had no time to contemplate them, for Vritrasura raised his mighty trident and sent it hurtling toward Indra, its prongs ablaze with fire so bright that no one could bear to look at it. Indra was not in the least discomfited; he was a deadly warrior who had the mightiest weapon of all. Indra flung his Vajra at the trident, which shattered into a thousand pieces, but so powerful was Indra's cast that the Vajra continued its flight and severed Vritrasura's right arm. Roaring with pain and anger, Vritrasura lashed out at Indra and Airavata with his left hand. God and elephant alike staggered with the force of the blow, which made Indra drop his Vajra. When Indra recovered from Vritrasura's attack, he saw the Vajra lying there on the ground, and he was ashamed of having dropped it.

"O Indra, why do you not take up your Vajra?" Vritrasura said. "Surely it is your purpose to use it to slay me. Pick it up, and let us continue our fight. I, for one, do not fear defeat. Defeat and victory are part of life, and no one can avoid one in favor of the other. Besides, fate decides for us what the outcome should be, and our fates are in the hands of the great Purusha who created and maintains all the worlds. One should always face life knowing this, and one should always face life with equanimity. You may have cut off my arm, O Indra, but that does not mean the battle is over.

"And I can fight you with equanimity, knowing that there is wisdom in releasing oneself from the tyranny of opposites. Life and death, wealth and poverty, illness and health are all part of life, and it is a wise being who understands that what we receive is willed by fate and out of our control. The *gunas*, the qualities of nature that are made of *sattva* (purity), *rajas* (activity), and *tamas* (destruction), are but natural things, and one who achieved release from the tyranny of opposites will never be enslaved by them.

"You have cut off my arm, Indra, but I will continue this fight. My fate is to fight you until one of us dies. Our mutual fate is to fight not knowing what the outcome might be. Let us finish our battle, and fight our best, for this is what is ordained for us to do."

Indra heard Vritrasura's words and was amazed by the wisdom of the great and fearsome Ashura.

Indra put his hands together in a show of respect for his enemy and said, "O my noble enemy, you are truly a *siddha* and an enlightened being. I salute your wisdom and your devotion to the Lord."

And so, Indra and Vritrasura once again took up their battle. Vritrasura cast his mace at Indra with his left hand, but Indra parried it with the Vajra and, in the process, severed Vritrasura's other arm from his body. Wounded as he was, Vritrasura did not give up the fight. He opened his mouth wider and wider until it seemed that he would swallow the whole world, and when his mouth was a great, gaping maw, he flung himself and Indra and swallowed him whole, along with the elephant Airavata. The Devas cried out in dismay when they saw that Vritrasura had devoured Indra, but the battle was not finished. From within the belly of the great beast, Indra wielded his Vajra, slashing open Vritrasura's belly. Indra and Airavata emerged from Vritrasura's belly and beheaded him with the Vajra.

The army of the Devas erupted into cheers, praising Indra for his great victory. But soon, the Devas became silent in astonishment, for the body of the dead Ashura began to glow with a holy light. The light rose into the sky and then dissipated, and thus all knew that Vritrasura had been released from the cycle of death and rebirth.

Now, even before Indra had heard the wisdom of Vritrasura on the field of battle, he was not sure he wanted to kill the demon, even though all the Devas were urging him to do it quickly.

Indra sought the counsel of the Rishis, saying, "When I killed Vritrasura's brother, I had to perform a year's penance, and I only was released from that penance when others agreed to assume it for me. What will happen if I kill yet another Brahmin? Vritrasura may be a demon, but surely there will be a price to pay if I slay him."

The Rishis replied, "It is of no matter. We will perform the *aswamedha yagna*, the horse sacrifice that will expiate your sin, and if you sing the many names of God, that also will absolve you."

Indra, therefore, went into battle and killed Vritrasura, but when he went home afterward, the sin of Brahmin-killing followed him, assailing him with worry during the day and terrifying dreams at night. Finally, Indra fled. He went to a lake and hid within the stem of a lotus. There he waited for a thousand years, and he suffered the whole time, for he could not receive the nourishment of the burnt offerings that were made to him. For a thousand years, Indra fasted and prayed to Vishnu.

When the Rishis found out where Indra had hidden, they performed the horse sacrifice on his behalf. And so it was that through fasting, prayer, and sacrifice, Indra was freed from his sin and resumed his throne.

Yayati and Devayani

This tale from the Bhagavata Purana *encapsulates many traditional Hindu values, including filial piety, fidelity to the Dharma, and the value of renouncing the flesh. When Prince Yayati finds himself caught between respecting his father-in-law's wishes and following the Dharma, he chooses the latter, bringing his father-in-law's curse down upon himself. But the curse, which causes instant old age, can be transferred to another willing person. When Yayati asks his sons to become old in his place, only Puru declares that obeying one's father is the most important thing, and so becomes an old man so that Yayati can retain his youth. Eventually, Yayati tires of living a life of bodily pleasure; he leaves his palace to become a hermit in the forest, and his wife follows his example.*

It is important to note that at no time is Yayati shamed for wanting a life of pleasure; instead, this is seen as one transitory phase of his life among many other phases. It is understood that he will give it up when he is ready and thus receive the rewards that accompany that renunciation. Likewise, Yayati's sons who refused to take on the old-age curse are not punished because their reasons for refusing it are seen as valid. Even so, the highest reward given to Yayati's children is reserved for Puru, who was the only obedient son, and who therefore has merited a position of authority over his brothers.

Vrishaparva was king of the Ashuras, and he had a daughter named Sharmishtha. Shukra was the guru to Vrishaparva, and he also had a daughter, whose name was Devayani. Sharmishtha and Devayani were good friends. They went everywhere together, and it was rare that you would see one of them outside the company of the other. One day, Devayani and Sharmishtha took a stroll down to the river. The sun was hot, and the day was fine, so they decided to swim in the cool water. They laid their clothing on the riverbank and then began to splash and play in the water.

As they were playing, they spied Lord Shiva coming toward them, riding his bull, Nanin, with his wife, Parvati, seated in front of him. The girls were anxious not to be caught naked in the water by the god, so they hurried out of the water to get dressed. Sharmishtha got to the riverbank first, and in her haste, she accidentally put on Devayani's clothes instead of her own. Devayani was livid when she saw the other girl wearing her garments.

"How dare you!" Devayani cried. "How dare a mere Ashura put on the clothes of a Brahmin! You have tainted my garments, and now I can no longer wear them!"

"Fancy the daughter of a beggar complaining about how I, the daughter of a king, happened to have taken her garments by mistake!" Sharmishtha said. "Brahmin your family might be, but you are beggars and nothing but. Your father is a servant to my father, and so you are a servant to me. Brahmin indeed!"

Then Sharmishtha picked up Devayani's clothing and pushed Devayani into a well that stood nearby. Sharmishtha returned home, where she told no one of what had happened on the riverbank.

Not long after Devayani had been pushed into the well, a young king named Yayati came riding along the very spot on the riverbank where Devayani and Sharmishtha had quarreled. Yayati had been out hunting all day, and he was tired and thirsty. He heard the sound of sobbing coming from nearby, so he dismounted and looked for who might be in distress. He looked down into the well, and there he saw Devayani, naked and sobbing.

"Who are you, and how did you get down there?" Yayati asked.

"I am the daughter of Shukra, who is guru to the Ashuras," Devayani replied. "Please help me. Pull me out of this well."

The young man took off his cloak and tossed it down to Devayani. Then he reached down into the well and pulled her up onto the riverbank.

"Thank you for rescuing me," Devayani said. "Please tell me who you are and where you are from, for it is fated that you should be my husband."

Yayati replied, "I don't see how that would be possible. I am only a warrior, a Kshatriya, while you are Brahmin. It is forbidden to marry someone outside one's caste."

"Yes, it is forbidden, but I am under a curse that I may never marry a Brahmin. Besides, I saw Lord Siva ride by today, and that is a sign that he wants us to be man and wife. Come to me again when my father sends for you."

The young people gazed into one another's eyes and realized they loved each other.

"I will come when your father summons me. Until then, farewell," Yayati said.

Then he mounted his horse and rode away to his city. Once Yayati was gone, Devayani collapsed at the foot of a tree and resumed weeping.

The sun had nearly set when Devayani heard the voice of her father calling to her.

"I am over here, father," she said, and Shukra came running to her side.

"Where have you been, my daughter?" Shukra asked. "I have been worried all day and wondered where you had gone when Sharmishtha came home by herself."

"Don't speak that demon's name to me ever again," Devayani said, and then she told her father all that had happened that day. When she had finished her tale, Devayani said, "I will never go back to Vrishaparva's court. Sharmishtha said such dreadful things about you, calling you a beggar and a flatterer. I want nothing to do with her or with her father."

"Is there no way you can come back with me, for my sake?" Shukra asked. "You needn't see Sharmishtha ever again. Her father and I can see to that. Come now, be kind and generous, and even if you cannot forgive Sharmishtha, at least do not hold her father to account for something he did not do."

"I know that Vrishaparva is innocent of this, but every time I see him, I will be reminded of his foul daughter and what she did to me. I will not go back to his court. I will not even set foot inside his city. I would rather die."

Shukra then took his daughter to a place where she might be sheltered and clad, and then he went back to Vrishaparva's palace.

"O Vrishaparva," Shukra said, "I am afraid I must leave your service. Your daughter insulted my Devayani quite unforgivably today, and she refuses ever to set foot in your city again. I cannot live without my daughter, so therefore I must leave."

When Vrishaparva heard this, he became very frightened.

"O Shukraguru," he cried, "please do not leave me! It is only by your grace that I hold my throne. What would I do without you? How can I appease your beloved daughter? Please take me to her that I might ask her forgiveness."

"I will take you, but I will only stay with you on the condition that you perform whatever penance she demands of you."

"It shall be done thus. Now please, take me to her right away!"

Shukra took Vrishaparva to the place where Devayani was waiting.

Vrishaparva fell at the young woman's feet and cried, "O Devayani, I beg your forgiveness for the insult my daughter did to you. Your father's wisdom is everything to me, and I have come to ask what I might do to make amends."

Devayani replied, "This is what you must do: When I am married, you must give me your daughter to be my servant. And all your daughter's servants must come with her, and they must serve me instead."

"It shall be as you say," Vrishaparva said.

Devayani told her father about Yayati, and Shukra agreed that it was an auspicious match. The wedding was joyous, and Vrishaparva kept his word; he brought Sharmishtha and one thousand other maidens to be Devayani's servants.

When the celebrations were over, Shukra said, "Sharmishtha has been given to be your wife's servant. She is not yours to do with as you please. You will not touch her."

"I give you my word that I will not," Yayati said.

Yayati and Devayani lived happily together, and soon Devayani found herself with child. Sharmishtha was jealous that Devayani was soon to be a mother, for she wanted children for herself.

Sharmishtha waited until the time when she knew she would be able to conceive, and then she went to Yayati and said, "I would be with child by you. Make love to me."

Yayati hesitated. Shukra had told him not to touch Sharmishtha, but Dharma demanded that he, as a Kshatriya, could not refuse a noblewoman who made this request, and besides, Sharmishtha was young and beautiful, and Yayati desired her. Yayati, therefore, lay with Sharmistha, and soon she was also with child. Devayani bore Yayati two sons, named Yadu and Turvasu. Sharmishtha brought forth three sons, named Druhyu, Anu, and Puru.

When Devayani found out that Yayati was the father of Sharmishtha's three sons, she fell into a rage. She roundly berated her husband and then stormed back to her father's house. Shukra also was angry with Yayati.

He went to the young king and said, "You promised not to touch Sharmishtha. You have disobeyed me, and therefore you shall be cursed with old age, right there as you stand."

"No, wait! Please wait!" Yayati cried. "I did not lie with Sharmishtha of my own desire. She demanded it of me, and the Dharma states that a Kshatriya cannot refuse a noblewoman when she asks this of him. I have not yet finished enjoying the pleasures of this life. Please do not do this to me!"

"Very well," Shukra said, who agreed that Yayati really had had no choice, "but my curse cannot be recalled. If you wish to retain your youth, you must find someone who is willing to give you theirs."

Shukra's curse took hold, and Yayati became an old man.

Yayati then went to his son Yadu and said, "Your grandfather cursed me to become an old man, but he said that if someone else gives me their youth, I can be young again. I am not yet ready to give up the pleasures of youth. Give your youth to me."

Yadu replied, "That I cannot do. I have only begun to experience the pleasures of youth myself. You will have to ask someone else."

Yayati went to Turvasu, Druhya, and Anu in turn, begging them to give him their youth, but they all refused.

Yayati then went to Puru and said, "O my son, you are my last hope. Please give me your youth so that I can finish enjoying the pleasures this world has to offer."

Puru replied, "How can a son refuse his father's request? The best son waits upon his father and anticipates his desires. The next best son does everything his father tells him to do. The next best son after that does what he is asked but does it with ill temper. The worst son disobeys his father, and that son is worth less than the contents of a chamber pot."

Puru then took upon himself Yayati's old age, and Yayati's youth was restored to him, and he continued to enjoy the pleasures of this world.

Yayati ruled wisely and well. He sated himself with all the good things the world has to offer, and his wife Devayani only added to his happiness by devoting herself to her husband in body and soul.

Yayati also performed many sacred rites and sacrifices, and he gave freely to temples, ashrams, and holy men. In this way, he faithfully worshipped Lord Hari, who in his person embodies all Vedas and all Devas, and who banishes all sorrows and receives all sacrifices. As Yayati devoted himself more and more to worship, he began to drift away from the life of the senses and began fixing his mind and heart upon the holy Vasudeva, the one who dwells within, and upon the holy Narayana, which he did without thought of blessings for himself.

Now, before Yayati reached that point, he had indulged his every desire for a thousand years, and it was not until a thousand years had passed that he began to yearn for things beyond the world of the senses.

He, therefore, went to his wife Devayani and said, "My wife, I wish to tell you a tale about a ram. This ram lived a good life, happy and free in the forest. One day, he came across a she-goat who had fallen into a well. The ram helped the she-goat out of the well. The she-goat saw what a fine ram it was that had helped her and so desired him. The ram mated with her, and because he was potent and virile, they were able to mate many, many times.

"The other she-goats saw how strong the ram was and how well he mounted the she-goat he had rescued from the well, and so they desired him. One of these other she-goats went to him, thinking to get his favors for herself. The ram lusted after this she-goat and so mated with her as well. This broke the heart of the she-goat the ram had rescued from the well, and she ran away to the home of the goatherd.

"The ram ran after his beloved she-goat, but when the goatherd understood how the ram had sinned, he took a knife and castrated the ram. But then the goatherd saw that this only made the she-goat more unhappy, so he restored the ram's testicles. The ram and the she-goat then recommenced with their mating and enjoyed one another over and over again, but still, this was not enough for the ram.

"I am just like that ram, O my wife. Just like him, I have chased after the pleasures of the body, and in doing so, I have set my soul aside and learned that indulgence never diminishes lust. It only increases it. Happiness cannot be found in the gratification of the senses but only in giving up all attachment. I, therefore, wish to renounce the life of the senses. I am leaving the palace, leaving this life of luxury, and even leaving you, O my wife, who I love most dearly. I shall live a life of poverty in the forest, among the animals and birds, and in this way, I hope to loosen the shackles of desire from my soul and to find enlightenment."

Yayati then gave his youth back to Puru and divided his kingdom among his sons. To Druhya, he gave the southeast, to Yadu, the south, to Turvasu, the west, and to Anu, the north, and he made Puru the emperor over all, with the other princes as his vassal kings. In this way, Yayati renounced the world of the senses and united himself joyfully with the Brahman, the ultimate reality of the universe.

For her part, Devayani took heed to her husband's tale and also gave up the material world in favor of the spiritual. She gave herself over to contemplation of the Lord, and in time, her physical body dissolved, and she achieved release from the cycle of death and rebirth.

Daksha and Shiva

Daksha is one of the Prajapati, *a collection of Hindu gods who assist with the process of creation and who are distinct from the single Vedic creator-god who is also called Prajapati. Hindu myth relates that one of Daksha's daughters, Sati, married the god Shiva against her father's wishes. In the story retold below, the conflict between Sati and Shiva and Daksha escalates because of Shiva's perceived slight against Daksha. The conflict leads to Sati immolating herself in protest.*

In traditional Hindu belief, the story of the war between Daksha and Shiva provides the rationale for the funerary practice that bears Sati's name—in which a living wife is immolated on the pyre of her dead husband. The practice of sati *(also sometimes spelled "suttee") was outlawed by the British in 1829 and has largely been abandoned in modern times. Unfortunately, there are still occasional cases of women committing* sati *today, especially in rural areas where traditional beliefs and practices hold greater sway than in more urbanized places.*

There came a time when all the Devas and other divine beings gathered together to hold a great sacrifice. When Daksha arrived, he was as splendid as the sun, and all the other beings rose to do him honor, except for Brahma and Shiva. Daksha went to Lord Brahma and bowed to him, as was right and proper, and Brahma showed him to his seat. But Daksha had seen that Shiva did not stand to honor him, and Daksha was gravely affronted.

"This is an offense to all propriety," Daksha said. "Everyone here rose when I entered, as is courteous, but this arrogant one retains his seat. He of all people should have risen, seeing that I am his father-in-law, and because of that, I am due respect from him. I never should have allowed my Sati to marry him. I now see that giving her to him was as much an offense and a waste of effort as it would be to teach the Vedas to a Shudra.

"This Shiva lives in funerary places with ghosts and demons, his hair always matted in *jatas* (dreadlocks), his body always smeared with the ashes of the cremated dead. He wears necklaces made from skulls and bones, and although his name is Shiva, the auspicious one, I say he is *ashiva*, the inauspicious. I only gave my precious daughter to him because my honored father Brahma asked me to, but now I regret that act. Sati deserves better than this lord of ghosts and ghouls!"

Daksha then took water in his hands and sipped it in a ritual fashion. Then he said, "Shiva, I curse you. From now on, when sacrifices are offered to the gods, you will not get your share. Your share will be divided among the other gods, and they shall have it for their own."

All the other gods gasped in astonishment at Daksha's curse since such an act was prohibited in the place of sacrifice, but Daksha merely turned on his heel and strode away, returning to his home.

Nandishwara, the guardian of the gate of Shiva's home on Mount Kailasa, heard Daksha's curse and became furious. He pronounced a curse upon Daksha in turn and upon all Brahmins who approved of Daksha's actions.

"For cursing my Lord Shiva, may Daksha and his followers bear my curse in return," Nandishwara said. "Anyone who thinks of Lord Shiva as does Daksha is no better than an animal, spending his life satisfying his bodily appetites. Therefore, Daksha shall have the head of a goat from henceforth.

"And those Brahmins who think that Daksha's curse was warranted shall from henceforth be chained to the cycle of birth, death, and rebirth. You will faithfully chant the Veda and follow its rituals, but your practice will be hollow, and you will have no understanding of the meaning of the scriptures. You will travel the world begging for your sustenance and eat whatever is given you, no matter how impure. That is my curse upon you!"

When the sage Bhrigu heard Nandishwara's curse, he rose in turn to curse him and the followers of Shiva.

"Anyone who follows the brigand Shiva is now cursed as a heretic! May they live among the bones and ashes with their master and wear their hair in matted *jatas* pierced with the bones of the dead. They shall be drunkards and outcasts, unclean and shunned by right-thinking people everywhere. No longer will they worship Lord Vishnu. Shiva shall be their only god, the lord of the goblins and demons!"

While Bhrigu was pronouncing his curse, Shiva rose from his seat with a sigh and quietly left the place of sacrifice with his followers. When Shiva and his followers left, the Devas and other blessed ones who remained completed the sacrifice. Then they went to bathe in the sacred waters of the holy place, where the flows of the Ganga and Yamuna meet, before going to their homes.

Many years passed following the sacrifice at which the curses were pronounced. In this time, Brahma made Daksha the chief of all the Prajapatis. Daksha became very prideful because of his elevation, and his hatred of Shiva continued to simmer in his heart. It came time for the sacrifice known as *brihaspati sava* to be performed. Daksha made all the arrangements and invited all the Devas and other holy beings to come to the sacrifice. All except for Shiva and Sati.

Sati heard that her father was preparing the sacrifice and saw the holy beings flying to where the sacrifice was to be held, all of them dressed in their best finery and decked out with jewels.

Sati said to Shiva, "My father is holding a great sacrifice. Everyone is going. I would like to go, too, and see my mothers and sisters. Let us go to the sacrifice as well. I know that you will say that we should not go because we have not been invited, but does a daughter need an invitation to visit her parents, or a son-in-law to go with his wife to visit them? Please, let us go. I have not seen my mother or sisters in so long, and it would make me so happy."

Shiva smiled and said, "My beloved wife, I know you miss your family. But I think that we should stay home. Your father still hates me, and now that he has been made chief of all the Prajapatis, his pride has increased all the more. I will not go to someone's home if they don't want me there because that is not the right thing to do.

"I know that it hurts you that your father cursed me and that he has not invited us to the sacrifice. Your father imagines that I slighted him when I did nothing of the sort. One should never bow to the body, but only to the divinity that lives within it, and one should never bow except to a superior. Your father forgets that he is not superior to me and that had I bowed to him, I would have been committing a sin for which I would have had to do penance. Your father cursed me, and so we are now enemies. I cannot send my wife to the home of my enemy, even if my wife also happens to be my enemy's daughter. No, beloved, we must stay home."

Sati felt angry and betrayed. Her eyes filled with tears. She loved Shiva and wanted to obey him, but she also loved and missed her family.

Shiva could sense her inward struggle and said, "O my wife, if you go to that sacrifice, the only outcome will be death. You will not be seen there as Daksha's daughter but as Shiva's wife, and that will put you in danger."

Sati wept tears of sadness and anger. She stormed out of the house, only to return, and then stormed out and returned again, so torn between going to the sacrifice and staying home as Shiva had bid her. But finally, her desire to see her family won out. She left the house and started to make her way to the sacrifice. Many of Shiva's followers went with her as an escort, as did Nandishwara, who insisted that Sati ride there upon Nandin, Shiva's sacred bull. Shiva, for his part, remained at home, feeling very sad.

When Sati arrived at the place of sacrifice, she looked to her father to see whether he would greet her, but he acted as though she weren't even there, and the other Devas followed his example. Only Sati's mother and sisters greeted her, which they did with much joy, for they had missed Sati as much as she had missed them. But Sati paid them no heed because she was so angry with her father for ignoring her.

Then Sati looked around the place of sacrifice and realized that none of the offerings were intended for Shiva. Sati finally understood that refusing to invite her beloved husband to the sacrifice was the least of Daksha's offenses on this day since he also intended to deny Shiva the sacrifices that were his due. The followers of Shiva who had accompanied Sati also saw this and prepared themselves to destroy the sacrifice, but Sati gave them one look, and they subsided, waiting for her orders about what to do next.

Sati smoldered with anger. She berated her father despite being in such a rage that she could barely speak.

"How dare you?" she said. "How dare you insult Lord Shiva thus? You have become so jealous and petty and prideful that you forget the truth, that Shiva is the lord of the universe, and only a fool would forget this.

"There are three kinds of people. The worst kind is the one who sees only the faults in others and none of the good. The one in the middle sees both the faults and the good. The best man sees only the good and overlooks the faults.

"You, however, are worse than even the worst person. You look at Shiva, the greatest of us all, and see only faults, while Shiva knows that you have cursed him and does not even hate you in return. Shiva might be able to bear your insults, but I cannot bear them. You called my husband *ashiva*, but it is you, Daksha, who are *ashiva*.

"When the follower of a god hears his beloved deity insulted, he should either cut out the tongue of the one who has made the insult or at the very least walk away from that evil person. But the true devotee of a god will not even wish to continue living once their deity has been insulted. I am such a person. You have insulted my Shiva, my husband and my god, and I no longer wish to live."

Sati gathered her golden robes about her and sat upon the ground. She closed her eyes and went into a yogic trance. She called the god of fire into her body and begged him to consume her. With one flash of flame, Sati's body was consumed, and all that was left in its place was a pile of ashes.

All of the Devas cried out in grief as they saw the flame go up, but none cried louder than Daksha.

Then the Devas said, "Oh, this is most inauspicious, not only that Daksha dared to insult the Lord Shiva but that he took no steps to prevent his daughter from immolating herself because of it! Many bad things surely will follow from these acts!"

When the followers of Shiva saw that their mistress had killed herself rather than see her husband insulted, they grasped their weapons. They surged toward Daksha, thinking of slaying him and then destroying the sacrifice in revenge. But Bhrigu saw them coming. He chanted a mantra against them and offered an oblation to the sacred fire. Out of the fire rose a host of spirits called Ribhus, who had prepared for battle by drinking sacred *soma*. The Ribhus had swords made out of holy fire, and with these, they attacked the followers of Shiva, who fled in all directions.

Among those followers of Shiva who had fled the sacrifice was the sage Narada. Narada went trembling and weeping before Lord Shiva and told him everything that had happened at the sacrifice. Shiva was not surprised at all; he had been expecting something like this, which is why he had told Sati not to go. But Shiva's sorrow over his wife's death was eclipsed by his rage at Daksha. Shiva took a strand of hair from his jatas and threw it to the ground with a great roar. Out of the strand erupted a creature of fire, the giant and fearsome Virabhadra, who had three eyes, a thousand arms, and hair made out of tongues of flame. His fangs were long and sharp, around his neck was a necklace of skulls just like Shiva's, and each of his hands held a weapon.

"What does my lord command?" Virabhadra asked.

"Go to the place where Daksha is holding the sacrifice," Shiva replied. "Take my followers with you. Kill Daksha. Destroy the sacrifice. Do it now."

Virabadhra made a *pradakshina* around Shiva, the sacred walking circle that would allow him to absorb Shiva's holy power. Then he gathered up the army of Shiva's followers, and with a roar, he departed for the place where Daksha was holding the sacrifice.

Now, once Bhrigu had banished Shiva's followers, Daksha and the others resumed their sacrifice. The ritual was finally continuing as it should when everyone noticed a great cloud of dust on the northern horizon.

"What is that?" some said.

"There isn't any wind, and it's not the season for storms," others said.

Yet others said, "Maybe the end of the world is coming?"

Daksha's wife, Prasuti, rightly guessed that the great cloud of dust was Shiva's wrath about to be visited upon her husband and all the Devas who supported him.

"My husband did very ill when he insulted Lord Shiva," she said, "and he did even worse when he drove our dear Sati to immolate herself. This is Shiva's vengeance for those affronts."

Within moments, the sacrificial hall was swarming with the followers of Shiva. They pulled down pillars, scattered the sacrificial fire and urinated in the firepit, smashed the holy utensils, and assaulted the priests and the wives of the Devas. They took Bhrigu and many other sages and Devas captive while Virabhadra sought out Daksha to kill him. Virabhadra laid hold of Daksha and cast him to the ground. He tried to cut off Daksha's head with one of his swords, but the blade would not cut the son of Brahma. Virabhadra then cast his weapons aside and strangled Daksha with his bare hands. When Daksha was dead, Virabhadra ripped his head off and tossed it into one of the pits that still burned sacred fire.

Shiva's followers cheered when they saw Virabhadra kill Daksha. Then they fell upon the great piles of food and drink that had been prepared for the celebration of the sacrifice. They ate until they were bursting and forced themselves upon the women who had not been able to flee. When all this was done, Virabhadra lit the place of sacrifice on fire and burned it to the ground. Then he and the rest of

Shiva's army returned to Shiva's home to tell him that Daksha had been slain and what else had befallen in their raid.

Now, those who had survived the raid made their way to Lord Brahma and Lord Vishnu, neither of whom had attended the sacrifice. They showed Brahma and Vishnu their wounds and told them all that Virabhadra and the others had done.

Brahma and Vishnu listened to the whole tale, then Brahma sighed and said, "Daksha was my son, but he was very foolish. He arranged that sacrifice solely to spite Shiva, which was badly done. A sacrifice once begun must be completed, or there will be terrible consequences, but worse still will be the consequences of Shiva's wrath over the death of his beloved Sati. You must all go to Kailasa and fall on your knees before Shiva. Beg his forgiveness. If he chooses to have mercy, then maybe he will not destroy the whole world in his wrath."

Then Yagna Deva, one of the holy beings who had come to ask for aid, said, "O holy Brahma, please come with us. Shiva's wrath is terrible, and maybe he is still angry with us."

"I will come because you ask me, but maybe Shiva will not be pacified even then," Brahma said.

And so it was that Brahma left his home in Satyaloka and went to Kailasa with the Devas and the others who needed to appease Shiva. They arrived at Shiva's holy mountain, and there they saw him seated under a sacred tree. Many great sages were seated around Shiva, and they were listening intently to a teaching he was giving them. When Shiva saw Brahma approach, he stood up and bowed to this lord of creation, and so did all of Shiva's companions.

Brahma said to Shiva, "Greetings to you, Lord Shiva, through whom the universe exists, and through whom things both begin and end. It was you who instituted the sacrifice, and it is you who rewards the souls of the righteous dead with bliss and punishes the wicked with eternal damnation.

"I come to you as the father of foolish Daksha, asking you to show him mercy and to have mercy upon these his followers. Bring Daksha back to life, as well as the others who were killed. Heal those who were wounded. Allow the sacrifice to be complete, and take all the sacrifice to yourself as your just dues."

When Shiva did not speak for a long moment, the Devas all began to tremble in fear.

But then Shiva laughed and said, "Lord Brahma, I am no longer angry, but it was necessary to punish Daksha so that he could let go of his vanity. He shall be restored to life, but he will have a goat's head from henceforth because Nandishwara's curse still holds. And let all who were wounded be healed."

When the Devas heard Shiva's words, they stopped trembling.

Then Brahma said, "Lord Shiva, please come with us to the place of sacrifice so that the ritual might be completed and you might restore life to those who perished."

Shiva did as Brahma asked. At the place of sacrifice, he put a goat's head on Daksha and restored him to life. Daksha looked at Shiva, and instead of hate and anger, he felt only love. He began to sing a hymn to Shiva, but as he did so, he remembered his dear Sati and began to weep instead.

He said to Shiva, "Lord, I have no words to express my gratitude. I treated you very ill and deserved my punishment, but you have forgiven me. Tell me how I might repay you, although I fear there is nothing that I can do that will be great enough."

Shiva replied, "I only ask that you complete the sacrifice, Daksha."

Just then, Lord Vishnu appeared, riding upon Garuda with his beloved wife, Lakshmi. Vishnu wore golden robes over his blue skin and a diadem that shone like the sun. Everyone present bowed to the three great gods who embodied the eternal Brahman, who created the universe and sustain it, and who will destroy it at the end of time.

It was then that Daksha was able to sing the praises of Shiva, and all the other Devas joined him, thanking him for his great mercy and lauding his greatness. Then Vishnu, Brahma, and Shiva blessed the sacrificial rite. Daksha rekindled the holy fire, and the sacrifice was completed as it was meant to be done. When it came time to divide the offerings among the gods, Daksha gave Shiva the first choice before distributing the rest to the others. After the sacrifice was completed, the gods all returned to their homes, and everyone was content, all except for Shiva.

Shiva entered his cave in the mountainside, and there he collapsed in grief. His beloved wife Sati was gone and would not return. Shiva mourned Sati until she was reborn as Parvati, the daughter of King Himavan and his wife, Mena. When the time was right, Shiva married Parvati. Shiva and Parvati loved one another, and they have remained married ever since.

The Defeat of Kaliya

The exploits of the god Krishna are many and are told in multiple sources. This particular tale from the Bhagavata Purana *recounts how Krishna defeated the great cobra, Kaliya, by dancing on the giant snake's hood. In addition to being a thrilling hero tale, this legend also functions as a just-so story, explaining why Indian cobras have markings on their hoods. These markings are said to be the imprints of Krishna's feet when Krishna danced on Kaliya's hood to defeat him.*

A long time ago, there was a deep place in the Yamuna River that held a cave, and inside the cave dwelled a great, venomous serpent named Kaliya. Kaliya's venom was so potent that when it seeped into the water, the water killed any creature that touched it, swam in it, or drank it. The poisonous fumes that rose from the water created a deadly, invisible miasma that hung above the river. Anything that breathed this deadly air died instantly. Birds that flew through it plummeted straight onto the earth or into the river. Cattle that inhaled even one small breath of it collapsed and died. The plants for miles around shriveled up and crumbled into dust whenever the miasma touched them. It was a most terrible thing, and worst of all was that when the wind shifted, it carried the poisonous air with it. It killed many others a far distance from the river who had no warning that death would take them on their very next breath.

One day, Krishna's cowherds took the god's cattle out to graze. Little did they know that the waters of the lovely Yamuna and the lovely breeze that played among the grasses and trees would soon mean their end. One light zephyr came from above the place where Kaliya lived, carrying the deadly fumes with it. As soon as the miasma reached them, Krishna's cattle and all of his dear cowherd friends died instantly.

Krishna mourned his cattle and his friends, and then he became angry. He decided that he would find the source of this menace and destroy it once and for all. He learned that it was Kaliya's venom that was poisoning everything for miles around. He found where along the river Kaliya's cave was. Near this place was a great kadamba tree whose limbs reached out over the water and which had not succumbed to Kaliya's venom because the holy Garuda had once perched in that tree. Krishna climbed the tree and worked his way down one great branch that grew directly over the place where Kaliya lived. Krishna secured his clothing more tightly about himself and then struck his arms with his hands to signal that he was challenging Kaliya to a fight. Then Krishna dove off the tree branch and into the roiling water. The impact of Krishna's body made a great splash that sent sheets of water straight up into the air and enormous waves surging over the banks of the river.

Krishna surfaced and began swimming toward Kaliya's den, with strokes so powerful that they seemed to be made by a great elephant. Beautiful was Krishna on that day, clad in golden clothing, his skin a piercing blue, the mark of the *srivatsa* on his chest, his face calm and smiling. But the great serpent Kaliya cared nothing for Krishna or for his beauty. When the evil serpent heard Krishna dive into the water, he came swimming up out of his den and shot straight for the young god. Kaliya wound his black coils round and round Krishna's body. Then Kaliya struck Krishna over and over with his fangs, wounding him in many places.

Krishna's friends, who had stayed away from the river that day, wondered where Krishna and the other cattle and cowherds had gone, too, so they took their herds and went looking for them. They arrived at the banks of the river just in time to see their god dive off the branch and be ensnared in the coils of the great, black serpent. When they saw Kaliya strike Krishna, and the bodies of the other cattle and cowherds strewn along the riverbank, they all cried out in horror. They were sure that Krishna would soon be dead just as those lying on the ground were. Even the living cattle mourned, lowing their grief as their cowherds wept.

Krishna's foster-mother Yasodha came running down to the river. When she saw her beloved foster-son in the coils of the snake, she screamed and ran toward the water as if to try to rescue her boy.

The others held her back, saying, "Nay, Mother, you would only die yourself. Wait here with us, mourn here with us."

Krishna's brother Balarama had also come down to the riverbank.

He said, "Have no fear. Krishna is not dead. It would take more than a little venom from a snake to kill him. Just watch."

Now, Krishna had been wounded badly by Kaliya's venom, which for the moment had made him unable to fight back. But when Krishna heard Balarama's encouraging words, he roused himself and, gathering all his strength, made his body swell and grow. Kaliya hissed and reared his great head above Krishna's body, venom spurting from his nostrils as he opened his great hood that was studded with rubies.

But Kaliya's strength was no match for Krishna's, and Krishna was not afraid of his deadly foe. Krishna broke free of the snake's coils and then swam around and around Kaliya, faster than the eye could see. Kaliya kept his eye trained on Krishna, his hood open, his head swaying around and around as he waited for Krishna to slow down so that he could strike. Krishna didn't slow. He swam like lightning around and around, and soon Kaliya became dizzy trying to follow the movements of the god. Krishna knew the moment had come. He slowed down and came within the great serpent's reach, but Kaliya's strike was slow and weak because he was too dizzy to strike properly. Krishna dodged out of the way of the great snake's fangs and put his powerful arms around the snake's neck just behind its head. Pushing Kaliya's head down toward the water, Krishna leaped up and onto Kaliya's open hood.

And what did Krishna do then—he began to dance! At first, there was no music but that of his feet as they trod the serpent's hood. But soon, he was joined by divine musicians who played sweet music from every instrument, sang divine songs, and danced along with Krishna. The power of Krishna's dance was such that blood began to seep out of Kaliya's eyes, and his body became weaker and weaker even as his hood remained open.

As Krishna danced, flowers began to fall out of the sky all around him. Kaliya became weaker and weaker, and soon thought that he was about to die, but then he realized who it was that danced upon his good.

"My Lord." The great serpent hissed. "Cease your dance, I beg you, for if you do not, I will surely die! I throw myself on your great mercy. Please, cease your dance!"

Kaliya's wives and children came swimming up out of their cave. They, too, begged for Kaliya's life.

"Please, Lord, do not kill Kaliya! We do not know how we will live without him!" they cried.

Then they began to sing a hymn to Krishna, saying, "You do justly when you punish those who do evil. It is right that you should dance upon Kaliya's head, for by doing so, you bless him through the expiation of his sins. Yes, Kaliya is a serpent, and venom is in his nature and in his body, for you have made him thus.

"We sing to you, and we bless you, O most divine one, for you are omniscient and omnipotent, all wisdom resides in you, and the Vedas spring from you. Any creature would count itself most fortunate to have but one touch of your feet, and Kaliya has been blessed with many. Please, bless him once more with your mercy. Bless us with your mercy. We need our husband, and our children need their father. Forgive Kaliya for not knowing who you were and how to do good. Now that he has been blessed by your dance let him have the chance to redeem himself so that he can come back to us."

No sooner had Kaliya's wives and children ceased their hymn than the great Kaliya collapsed. Krishna ceased his dance and waited. When Kaliya came to, he looked into the god's eyes with love.

"O Blessed One," Kaliya said, "I know now who you are, and I know the nature of my sin. That sin was inbred in me, for you have created us serpents to be fierce and venomous. Only you can save us from our natures, and I humbly ask your forgiveness."

Krishna said to Kaliya, "You are forgiven, but you cannot stay here. People and cattle and all manner of other creatures need to use the river and its water. You need to go back to the ocean, where you came from, and your wives and your children need to go with you."

Then Krishna said, "From now on, anyone who hears the story of how I vanquished Kaliya will never be afraid of snakes. Anyone who comes to this place on the river to bathe in the water where I danced on your hood will be freed from all sins. And your hood, Kaliya, and those of all your kind will now bear the sign of my dancing feet. This sign will make Garuda and all other eagles afraid of you, and they will not molest you anymore."

Kaliya and his wives and children then gave many precious gifts to Krishna. They worshiped him and bowed to him.

Then Kaliya said, "With your leave, Lord, we will now go back to the island of Ramanaka in the ocean, and we will live there, as you have bid us do."

"You have my leave," Krishna said, and so Kaliya and his family went back to their old home.

Never again was the river Yamuna tainted with venom, and its waters flowed free and clear for the good of all the creatures of the earth.

Part II: Tales from the Mahabharata

The Story of Shantanu

The story of King Shantanu opens the epic Mahabharata, *laying down the genealogical point of origin for the two sets of cousins whose feud is at the core of the epic's conflict. The story also explains the divine origins of Bhishma, Shantanu's son and one of the main heroes of the* Mahabharata, *whose mother is none other than Ganga, the goddess of the divine Ganges River herself.*

Oaths taken and then kept or broken, and the consequences that follow from those actions, are at the heart of this tale, both for Shantanu and especially for his son, Bhishma. Shantanu is a complex character who wants to do right by his family, himself, and his subjects. He is a man of his word and tries hard to trust Ganga even when he sees her committing filicide—since he promised her he would never interfere with her or ask her questions. When at last Shantanu can no longer bear watching her kill yet another of their children, he loses his wife but later gains a son, Devavrata, who Shantana saves from being thrown into the river. Devavrata goes on to become the great hero Bhishma, gaining that epithet when he makes a terrible vow to renounce his throne and remain celibate ("Bhishma" means "terrible" in Sanskrit, in the sense of "inducing terror"). As we see here and in the story that follows, Bhishma's steadfastness in keeping his vow has repercussions not only for himself but for many other people.

Shantanu and Ganga

Once there was a king of the Kurus named Shantanu. He was a young king, handsome and well made in his body. Hunting was his favorite pastime, and he spent much of his time in the forest with his bow and arrows, which he used to take down many fat deer and goats.

Although Shantanu knew that it was his duty to produce an heir to the throne, he had not yet married. Many kings had offered their beautiful daughters, but Shantanu had refused them all. This was because he had a recurring dream in which a beautiful woman appeared. Shantanu had fallen in love with this dream woman and so would have no other.

One day, Shantanu went out hunting as was his wont. He chased after game all day, but as fine an archer as he was, all his shots went awry. The sun had begun to set, but so intent was Shantanu on bringing down at least one animal that he pressed on, despite both he and his horse being weary. On they went until they came to the banks of the holy Ganga, and as Shantanu and his horse paused to slake their thirst, a beautiful woman appeared. She was tall and slender, dressed in the finest of silks, and bedecked with gold and jewels. Her long black hair was lustrous and fell to her waist, and her eyes were warm and inviting. Shantanu was so stricken by her beauty that he could not speak for a long moment, but he did not have to wonder who this woman was: She was the one who had been appearing in his dreams.

Shantanu finally spoke, "You are the woman for whom I have waited and loved these many years. I ask you to do me the honor of marrying me and being my wife."

The woman replied, "I also love you and will gladly be your wife, on one condition."

"You have but to name it, and I will surely do it."

"You must never question what I do or interfere with it, nor must you ever try to find out who I truly am. If once you break that promise, I must leave you forever."

"I promise that I will always do those things, for I could not bear to lose you."

And so it was that Shantanu and the woman from his dreams were married. Since Shantanu did not know her true name and could not ask it of her, he called her Ganga, after the name of the holy river where he had found her.

The young couple lived happily together, and after a time, Ganga announced that she was with child. Shantanu rejoiced at this since now he would have an heir to his throne and a child of his own to care for. When her time came, Ganga delivered a healthy baby boy, and Shantanu's happiness only increased. But on the night that the baby was born, Shantanu found himself unable to sleep and so sat near the open window of his chamber to look upon the moon and stars. He had only sat there for a moment when to his astonishment, he saw his wife hastening toward the river, her newborn babe in her arms. Shantanu ran out of the palace and followed her, but before he could catch up to her, he saw her lift the baby up toward the sky and then cast him into the rushing water. Shantanu cried out, but then his wife whirled around to face him, a fierce look on her face.

"Remember your oath," she said and then strode past him and went back into the palace.

Shantanu stayed by the river for some moments, weeping and trembling with fear and anger.

"Who is this woman that I have married?" he asked himself. "Is she some kind of demon? Have I put my life and my throne in jeopardy? Oh, alas for my little son, who did nothing to deserve that fate!"

Shantanu returned to the palace, and although he soon resumed normal relations with his wife, nothing was ever quite the same as before she had drowned their son. It was not long before Ganga was with child again, and again Shantanu dared rejoice, but on the night the child was born, Ganga again went down to the river and threw the baby into the water. Again, Shantanu followed her, and again he said and did nothing, remembering his promise. Five more times did Ganga get with child, and five more times did she throw the baby into the river on the night of its birth. Having thus lost seven children in a row, Shantanu vowed to himself that he would save the eighth, even if it meant losing his wife or even his life.

Ganga's Tale

The next time Ganga delivered a child, she went down to the river with the baby in her arms, as she had done seven times before. But this time, Shantanu went to the river to wait for her, and when she arrived bearing the infant, Shantanu shouted at her to stop.

"No more!" he cried. "No more will you throw defenseless infants into the water. No more murder. No more drownings. I can't let this go on. I intend to save that child if it is the last thing I ever do."

Ganga turned to Shantanu and smiled. "You have broken your promise to me, and now I must leave you. But no matter. At least the curse is ended now."

Shantanu was baffled by this. "What do you mean? What curse? Explain yourself!"

"I will tell you all, for you deserve to know. You call me Ganga because you found me near that holy river, but you must know that I am Ganga indeed, the daughter of Jahnu, and now you shall see me as I truly am."

Ganga then showed Shantanu that she was a goddess, and he fell on his knees before her.

Ganga resumed her tale, saying, "I came to earth and became your wife because of a curse that was laid upon the Vasus, the divine ones who wait upon Lord Vishnu. There was a time when the eight Vasus decided to walk the earth with their wives, and they found themselves in the field where the sage Vasishta grazed his beloved cow, Nandini. The Vasus and their women gazed at the cow, for they had never seen one as beautiful as she. Her coat was glossy and her flanks well rounded, and her udders full of milk so rich that it would restore health even to the sickest person.

"One of the Vasus's wives said, 'O my husband, take for me that cow. I must have her.'

"The Vasu replied, 'That I dare not do. The cow belongs to the sage Vasishta. If I take her, the sage will be very angry.'

"'I do not want the cow for myself,' the heavenly woman said. 'I want her for my friend, who is ill and dying. Just a little of this cow's milk will restore her to health.'

Hearing this, the other Vasus agreed that taking the cow was a needful act. Dyau, the husband of the heavenly woman who wanted to heal her friend, took the cow, and with her, the Vasus and their wives returned to their heavenly abode.

"When Vasishta went to the field that evening to fetch his cow, he was devastated to find her missing. He loved that cow more dearly than a mother loves its child. He also knew by his wisdom that it was the Vasus who had taken her, and Vasishta was terrible in his wrath. He thus cursed the Vasus, condemning them to be born into the world as mortals.

"The Vasus felt the curse strike them as soon as it was uttered, and they were in great distress. Living as mortals on the earth would mean that they would have to suffer pain and sickness and death, and they wanted none of those things. They raced down to Vasishta's ashram, bringing the cow with them, and flung themselves at his feet.

'O great Rishi,' they said. 'Here is your cow. Please withdraw your curse. We only took the cow so that a sick woman might be healed and not out of any thought of profit for ourselves.'

"Vasishta replied, 'Once a curse is pronounced, it may not be revoked. But there may be a way to make it less harsh. You must find a woman who is willing to be your earthly mother. Tell her that she must drown you in the river as soon as you are born. That way, you will have been born as mortals, but you will not have to suffer a mortal life.' Vasishta then turned to Dyau and said, 'But for you, who did the deed of stealing, you shall be condemned to serve out a full life as a mortal. You will have a good life, but it will still be a mortal one, for all that. Now, go and find someone who can be a mother to you on earth.'

Then Vasishta took his cow and went away from that place.

"The Vasus discussed who might be willing to become their mother on earth. They agreed that they should ask me, the goddess Ganga, so they came to me and fell at my feet. They told me about their deed and the Rishi's curse.

Then they said, 'Please, O Ganga, please be our mother on earth, and do as the Rishi said you might do.'

I agreed, and so it was that I appeared to you on the banks of the river, married you, and bore your children and threw them one by one into the water. And this infant that I hold now in my arms is Dyau, who must live out a mortal lifespan.

Her tale concluded, Ganga said to Shantanu, "But even though you now know why I did what I did, I cannot take you back as my husband. You broke your promise, and so I am lost to you forever, and I must keep our son with me, for an infant needs its mother."

Shantanu begged Ganga to stay, but she stood firm. Finally realizing that his pleas were of no use, Shantanu said a tearful farewell to his beloved wife and son. Then the goddess vanished, cradling her infant in her arms. Shantanu returned to his palace, where he ruled as wisely as he could, and he was a good king to his people. But for the next sixteen years, he gave no thought to taking another wife, for his heart still belonged to the river goddess.

Ganga Returns

One day, sixteen years after Ganga had disappeared with his son, Shantanu found himself wandering along the banks of the holy river. The flow of the water had slowed to a trickle, and Shantanu wondered who or what had made the river dry up. As Shantanu stood gazing at the miraculous dam, he suddenly realized he was not alone. He turned, and who should be standing beside him but his beloved Ganga!

When Shantanu had regained command of himself, he said, "You have come back to me at last. Woe that I am now an old man, but I rejoice at seeing you once more. I never thought you would return. Please tell me that you are here to stay and to be my wife once more."

Ganga smiled and said, "I am pleased to see you as well, but we can never live as man and wife again. That time in our lives has passed, and cannot be lived over again. But tell me, did you see the dam along the river?"

"Yes, indeed I did. Who made it?"

Before Ganga could answer, the dam cracked with a sound like a thunderclap, and the water came rushing through the gap with a roar.

As the flood of water subsided and the river returned to its accustomed bed, a beautiful young man came running up to Ganga and said, "Mother! I did it! I made the dam!"

Ganga said, "Yes, I saw that. Well done!" Then she looked from the young man to the old king and said, "Shantanu, do you know who this is?"

Shantanu studied the boy's face and then looked back at Ganga. "No, it can't be . . ."

"This is your son," Ganga said. "His name is Devavrata. He has been raised well and educated as a Kshatriya. He knows all the Vedas, having been taught by the Rishi Vasishta himself, and he has been trained in horsemanship and the use of all weapons by the greatest warriors in the world." Ganga turned to her son and said, "Devavrata, this is your father, King Shantanu."

Devavrata bowed to his father, but before he could say anything, Shantanu wrapped him in a tight embrace. "My son!" he cried. "I thought I would never see you again, and here you are, a young man and a warrior!"

"He is all that and more," Ganga said. "He is the heir to your throne. Take him with you, with my blessings upon both of you."

And with that, Ganga vanished, leaving father and son alone on the riverbank, where the waters flowed peacefully. Devavrata and Shantanu walked back to the palace together, delighting in one another's company and telling each other tales of what had passed during the years they were parted.

Shantanu and the Fisher-Girl

Four years passed after Devavrata was returned to his father. Shantanu formally named Devavrata his heir-apparent, and the youth was well beloved by all the kingdom's people. Devavrata was wise, just, considerate, and behaved toward his father as the perfect son ought to do. Shantanu was well content and thought his life surely was complete—although he did miss his beloved Ganga.

One day, Shantanu went out hunting. His charioteer drove the royal chariot, and they followed the game for a long way but had shot nothing. Soon they found themselves along the banks of the Yamuna River. Just as they paused to refresh themselves, Shantanu caught the scent of a subtle and bewitching perfume on the breeze.

"I must see where this perfume is coming from," Shantanu said.

So he bade the charioteer drive along the riverbank, following the trail of the scent.

Finally, they came to the hut of a fisherman. Mooring a small fishing boat to the dock in front of the house was the most beautiful young woman Shantanu had ever seen, and the scent he had followed was the young woman's own. Shantanu's heart was instantly pierced by love for this woman, and he decided that he must have her for his wife. Shantanu jumped out of the chariot.

He softly asked her, "What is your name?"

The young woman was startled, for she had neither seen nor heard Shantanu approach.

Again, Shantanu said, "What is your name? I am Shantanu, the King of the Kurus. You are so very beautiful. Will you do me the honor of being my wife?"

The young woman did not meet Shantanu's eye, but she replied, "My name is Satyavati. My father is the king of the fishermen on this river. My duty is to row this boat to ferry people from one side of the river to the other."

"Is your father here?"

"If he is, he is within our house," Satyavati said, pointing to the hut.

Shantanu went to the hut and knocked on the door.

When the fisherman answered, Shantanu said, "Greetings to you. I am Shantanu, the King of the Kurus. I was hunting today when I caught the scent of your daughter's perfume. I followed the scent all the way here and saw your daughter mooring her boat. I confess that I fell in love with her instantly and would like her to be my wife, with your permission, of course."

The fisherman replied, "My lord, you are welcome to my humble home. I wish you all joy and much peace, and long may you reign. But I cannot give my daughter's hand in marriage unless you promise to make her your queen and make her sons your heirs."

"That is a bold request."

"It is indeed, but I must make it because a holy Rishi told me that my daughter's son would become king of these lands. I will be happy to allow her to wed you, but only if you make her your queen and make her son your heir, as I have said."

Shantanu's heart sank within him. He badly desired Satyavati, but what would he tell Devavrata? The young man had already been invested as heir-apparent. He was young, brave, wise, and beloved of the people. How could Shantanu take his throne from him?

Shantanu could not find words to reply to the fisherman. He merely nodded sadly and then took his leave. After one last pining look at the lovely Satyavati, he returned to where his charioteer awaited him and went back to his palace with a heavy heart.

Devavrata's Vow

Shantanu's mood did not lift once he returned home. He became withdrawn and morose and refused even to see his beloved son. Devavrata saw this change in his father's behavior and became worried.

He went to his father and said, "My father, what is wrong? You no longer speak to me as you used to, you hide in your chambers all day, and you barely attend to affairs of state. What has happened to you that you behave this way?"

"You are right, Devavrata," Shantanu replied. "I have changed. It is because I am worried for the future of my kingdom. You are a warrior, a Kshatriya. It is your duty to fight to protect your kingdom. But what if something happens in battle and you are killed? You are my only son, the only heir to the kingdom.

"You mustn't think that I would marry another and so take your throne away from you. But I cannot help wondering what the future holds for my kingdom should you die before you take the throne yourself."

Devavrata listened carefully to what his father said and even more carefully to what was not being said. He soon realized that his father must have fallen in love again and that his wish to marry was at war with his love for his son.

Devavrata then went to his father's charioteer and said, "When you took my father out hunting the other day, where did you go, and what did you see?"

At first, the charioteer refused to answer, saying that it was not proper for him to tell anyone tales about where he took the king, not even the king's son. But Devavrata persisted.

Finally, the charioteer gave in and said, "We hunted our way to the banks of the Yamuna. There your father caught the scent of a bewitching perfume. We followed the scent along the river until we came to a fisherman's hut. The fisherman's daughter was mooring her boat at the dock in front of the hut. Your father saw how beautiful the young woman was and instantly fell in love. He asked for her hand in marriage, but her father said he would consent only if your father made the girl his queen and her son his heir. Your father has been troubled because he is very much in love with the fisher-girl, but he also loves you and does not want to deprive you of your throne."

At first, Devavrata was angry that the fisherman had denied his father, the king of the realm, his daughter's hand in marriage. But then Devavrata smiled.

He said to the charioteer, "Have no fear. No harm shall come to you because of what you have told me. I thank you for your honesty. Now, will you please take me to the fisherman's hut? I wish to speak with this man who dares to say no to the king."

The charioteer did as he was bidden.

As he and Devavrata got closer to the fisherman's hut, Devavrata caught the scent of the same perfume that had bewitched his father. Arriving at the fisherman's hut, Devavrata saw the young woman on the dock mooring her boat, just as Shantanu had first discovered her.

She is indeed beautiful, Devavrata thought, *and her scent is intoxicating. No wonder my father fell in love.*

Devavrata went up to the young woman and said, "Greetings. I am Devavrata, the son of King Shantanu, who asked for your hand some days ago. I would like to speak with your father, please. Can you show me to him?"

The young woman agreed and showed Devavrata to the hut, where the fisherman was cooking some fish for the midday meal.

The fisherman came outside and said, "Who are you, and what do you want?"

"Greetings," Devavrata said. "I am the son of King Shantanu, who asked for your daughter's hand in marriage. I understand you refused him, and I would like to know why considering the honor that would be bestowed on your daughter and on your family by your acceptance."

The fisherman bowed to the prince. "My lord, it is true that I denied your royal father's request, but it was not from pride or arrogance. A Rishi told me that it was my Satyavati's fate to marry a king and that her son would be the heir to the throne. I could not in good conscience grant your father's request."

"I see. Why did my father not consent to this condition and take your daughter?"

"Forgive my impertinence, my lord, but you are the crown prince, and you have to ask that question? Your father is in love with my daughter, true, but how could he deny the throne to his only son? King Shantanu had to make a choice, and his loyalty to you and love for you won out."

"If that is all that stands in the way of my father's happiness, then I renounce my throne."

The fisherman replied, "You are the perfect son to think principally of your father's happiness, and I honor you deeply for it. But I must ask: what of your own sons? Will there not be strife between Satyavati's children and your own once they are of age to take the throne?"

"If that is an obstacle, then I will be celibate. I will not marry, and I will not have sons. Then your grandson will be the heir, with no contention from me or from my own children, and the Rishi's prophecy will be fulfilled."

The fisherman frowned doubtfully. "Forgive me once more, my lord, but that is a great renunciation for one such as you to make. How will I know that you intend to keep your word and that you are not merely telling me what I want to hear so as to secure your own father's happiness?"

"I swear by all the gods, and especially by my own holy mother, Ganga, and by the Dharma, that I renounce my throne, shall never marry, and shall never sire any children. Does that satisfy you?"

Before the fisherman could reply, a radiant light glowed down from the sky, and a shower of flower petals came down on Devavrata. Faint, heavenly music played, and a breathtaking scent more fragrant than Satyavati's own filled the air.

Divine voices rang out, saying, "Bhishma! Bhishma!" because the vow Devavrata had taken was so holy and so terrible that it could never be broken.

Devavrata was forever after known as Bhishma.

The fisherman was awestruck, and at first, could not find his tongue. But then he beckoned his daughter to join them.

He presented Satyavati to Bhishma, saying, "My lord, greet your new mother. Take her to your father, and may they have a long and joyous life together."

Then without another word, the fisherman turned and went into his hut and closed the door. That night he died in his sleep, whether because the prophecy was finally fulfilled or from the grief of losing his only daughter, we shall never know.

Bhishma greeted Satyavati with great honor and showed her to the chariot. The charioteer brought them back to Hastinapura as fast as he could drive, with Bhishma constantly asking him to go faster, for he could not wait to bring Shantanu his bride and thus make his father happy again.

Soon they arrived at the palace, and Bhishma brought Satyavati to the king.

"My father," Bhishma said. "Behold, I bring you your bride. Put away your sorrow and rejoice that you have the woman you love!"

Shantanu could not speak at first. Then he stammered out, "My bride? But her father said— Oh, my dear son, my beloved Devavrata, what have you done?"

"I have renounced my throne, father, and I have made a holy vow never to marry nor to sire children. Satyavati is your wife, and her son shall sit upon the throne of Hastinapura."

Shantanu collapsed into a chair, overcome with guilt that his desire for Satyavati led Devavrata to renounce his throne and manhood.

When Shantanu was finally able to speak again, he said, "I know not what to say, my son, other than to thank you for your noble sacrifice. Even had your vow not been so holy, I would never ask you to go back on your word. Since you have given up so much that I may be happy, I will take your gift with much gratitude. I shall marry Satyavati, and I shall do my best to make our lives together full of joy. And because of this sacrifice, I grant you this blessing: that you may never die until such time as you so wish to die, and only then shall death take you."

Shantanu and Satyavati were wed in a joyous celebration. In time, Satyavati bore two fine sons, one named Chitraganda and the other Vichitravirya. Shantanu gave the duty of ruling the kingdom to Bhishma, for he was now an old man and wished to spend his last years enjoying his wife and children. Bhishma ruled wisely and well, and he saw to it that his two young half-brothers were taught the Vedas and the use of weapons and all other things that a Kshatriya and a prince should know. Bhishma was a loving elder brother, almost a second father to the two young princes, and it delighted Satyavati's heart that Bhishma loved her sons so well.

After many happy years with Satyavati and his children, Shantanu passed away. Bhishma continued to rule as regent since the two princes were as yet too young to take the throne themselves, but before Bhishma could relinquish that duty, tragedy struck.

When Chitraganda was a young man and nearly ready to be crowned king, a Ghandarva discovered a mortal who shared his name. The Ghandarva was outraged that anyone else would have the same name as he had. So he went to Hastinapura and challenged young Prince Chitraganda to a battle to see who would honor the name Chitraganda. The young prince was a proud Kshatriya and so could not refuse the challenge. He fought very well, but in the end, his strength and skill were no match for those of the divine Ghandara, and Chitriganda was killed.

Bhishma, therefore, continued to rule as regent until Vichitravirya was of age to take the throne. When the time came, the young prince was crowned in a great ceremony, and Hastinapura was well content with their new king. Vichitravirya ruled very well for some years, with Bhishma ever at his side to offer aid and counsel.

The Death of Bhishma

"Hell hath no fury like a woman scorned" is an oft-repeated phrase, and in the Mahabharata, the embodiment of that scorned female fury is Amba, the daughter of the king of Kasi. When Bhishma kidnaps Amba and her sisters so that they can marry his

younger brother, Bhishma only belatedly finds out that Amba intended to marry someone else. However, because Amba has been stolen by another Kshatriya, her intended now considers her to be damaged goods and spurns her. Bhishma will not marry her because of his vow, and Bhishma's brother declines her hand as well since she is in love with another man. Bhishma's precipitate and violent solution to acquiring a bride for his brother, therefore, has horrible, unforeseen consequences for Amba, and in turn, leads to Bhishma's death.

The ceremony interrupted by Bhishma is called a swayamvara. *It is an ancient Indian custom wherein the bride chooses what man she will marry by placing a flower garland around his neck. An auspicious time and place were chosen for the ceremony, and eligible men gathered with their families to see who the bride would choose. Once she made her choice, the wedding ceremony itself was held immediately. In the tale retold below, a royal family is holding the ceremony, but in ancient Indian practice, swayamvara was not confined to the upper classes.*

The Swayamvara

The kingdom of Hastinapura was prosperous and at peace. King Vichitravirya was just and generous, and his half-brother Bhishma advised him well. After a few years, Bhishma thought it was time that Vichitravirya should wed, for the kingdom needed an heir. It had been the custom for many generations that the king of Hastinapura would marry the daughter of the king of Kasi, and Bhishma expected that this custom would be upheld for Vichitravirya. But this was not to be; news came to Bhishma that instead, the king of Kasi was holding a swayamvara for his daughters so that they might choose their own husbands, and what was worse, Vichitravirya had not been invited because the king of Kasi thought the son of a fisher-girl too lowly to be his daughter's husband. Bhishma was dismayed and angered by this slight. He vowed to go to the swayamvara and take all three of the king's daughters to be brides for Vichitravirya.

When the day of the swayamvara came, all of Kasi was in a state of celebration. Garlands of flowers were strung everywhere, and no place was more beautifully decked out than the king's hall where the swayamvara was to take place for the king's daughters, who were named Amba, Ambika, and Ambalika. Princes from all the neighboring kingdoms were gathered in the king's hall, wearing their very finest clothing and jewelry, all hoping that one of the king's daughters would choose them to be her husband. When these princes saw Bhishma enter the hall, they sniggered, not hiding their contempt.

They whispered among themselves, saying things like, "Why is he here? I thought he had taken a vow never to marry? Isn't he a bit old? Then again, maybe these girls are so beautiful that even Devavrata can't help himself."

Bhishma heard what they said.

He stood in the hall of the swayamvara, a powerful Kshatriya, and said, "Yes, indeed I am come to this swayamvara, but not for myself. I come on behalf of my brother, King Vichitravirya, for it has been the custom for generations that the king of Hastinapura marries the daughter of the king of Kasi. And since you have slighted my brother not only by holding a swayamvara but also by not even inviting him here, I will take not one but all three of the princesses to be my brother's brides."

With that, Bhishma snatched up all three girls and jumped into his chariot.

He whirled to face the crowd of thunderstruck princes and the king of Kasi and said, "If any of you want one of these women for your own, come and take her, if you can. Come and fight me, and we'll see who shall be their husbands!"

Then Bhishma called to his charioteer, and off they raced, with the three young women too terrified to protest.

The princes all ran to their chariots and raced off after Bhishma. They drew their bows and shot arrow after arrow, but none found their mark. Bhishma raced on, but suddenly he turned his chariot around and began shooting himself, and every shot was true.

Now, among the suitors who had been invited to the swayamvara was a prince named Shalva. Shalva had come to the swayamvara because he loved Amba, the eldest princess, and had hoped that she would choose him. Shalva was the last remaining Kshatriya in the pursuit, and such was his skill that he managed to wound Bhishma with three arrows. Bhishma was stunned that a mortal man had been able to wound him, but such was his strength and courage that he merely plucked out Shalva's arrows and fired back, killing all of Shalva's horses and his charioteer. Shalva himself was flung to the ground, stunned and weaponless, but the honorable Bhishma refused to kill a man who was thus rendered helpless. Bhishma turned his chariot around once more and thundered off to Hastinapura, where the people welcomed him and the princesses of Kasi with cheers and showers of flower petals.

Amba's Plight

When Bhishma arrived at the palace, he led the three princesses to Satyavati's chamber.

"Look what I have brought, mother," Bhishma said. "I have three brides for Vichitravirya and daughters-in-law for you."

Satyavati looked at the three young women and was very pleased. She sent for Vichitravirya and showed him the brides Bhishma had brought for him. Vichitravirya was so grateful that he fell at Bhishma's feet in gratitude. Then he stood and embraced him.

Then Amba spoke, "Please, if I may?"

Bhishma replied, "Of course. You are in no danger. This is your home, and we are your family."

"My lord, when you came and whisked us away from the swayamvara, you prevented me from marrying the man I love. I intended to place my garland around Shalva's neck, for we love each other and wished to marry. I know not what to do now since you took us all away so abruptly."

"Why didn't you say so? If I had known, I never would have taken you."

"I was too afraid, and everything happened so quickly. I had not found the courage to speak until now."

There was an awkward silence that was only broken when Vichitravirya said, "If she loves another, I should not marry her. Bhishma, please return her to Shalva so that they may wed."

"What my brother says is right," Bhishma said to Amba. "We will see you safely to Shalva's palace, and we wish you well."

Amba smiled with joy and relief, and the others all smiled with her.

Satyavati said, "Let it be as Bhishma said. You should go to your Shalva and marry him with my blessing."

Bhishma arranged for a chariot and an escort of soldiers to take Amba to Shalva's kingdom. Amba was rapt with joy as she would soon marry the man she loved.

When she arrived, she went to Shalva and said, "My lord, I have returned to you. I was going to put my garland on you at the swayamvara, but Lord Bhishma took us all away before I could do it. I told Bhishma and his brother that I loved you and wanted you and only you, and they let me go with their blessing. My beloved Shalva, here I am, ready to be your bride."

Shalva laughed contemptuously. "Ready you may be, but you shall never be my bride. The Dharma says that when a Kshatriya takes a maiden in battle, she becomes his and only his. I'll not take Bhishma's castoffs to be my own. If you want to get married, go back and wed Bhishma, if he will have you."

Shamed and brokenhearted, Amba made her way back to Hastinapura.

She went to Bhishma and said, weeping, "Shalva will not have me. He says the Dharma demands that you and only you marry me."

Bhishma's heart filled with compassion for this young woman.

He said gently, "I am very sorry, but I cannot marry you. I made a solemn and holy vow that I would never wed and that vow I will not break. My heart weeps with yours for the sorrow I have caused you. If only you had said something when I took you in Kasi! But we are both bound by our fates. Only know that I would gladly have married you were I not constrained by my oath. Perhaps if you go back to Shalva and ask him once more, he will relent."

"That he will not. I know King Shalva well. He has nothing but contempt for me now. You had courage enough to snatch me and my sisters away from the swayamvara and fight a horde of suitors for us. Can you not find the courage to break your vow and marry me? Do not leave me without a husband."

Bhishma shook his head sadly. "It is not a matter of courage, my lady. I will not break my sacred vow, not for you, nor for any other woman. If you will not try to change Shalva's mind, then you are welcome to stay here in honor, as part of the royal household, and your every need shall be met."

Then Bhishma left while Amba wept bitterly.

At the Ashram

Amba spent six years at Vichitravirya's court, and every day was more painful than the last. She watched as her younger sisters married the king and lived happily as his wives while she remained alone. At the end of the six years, Amba's misery was such that she decided to ask Shalva once again whether he would have her, but he only spurned her with even greater venom than before, and once again, she returned to Hastinapurna weeping and ashamed.

Amba's anger against Bhishma grew and grew, for she blamed him for all her misery. Finally, she decided to go into the forest to see whether any of the Rishis who dwelled there might be enlisted to convince Bhishma to marry her. When she arrived at the ashram, the holy men who lived there prepared to turn her away when suddenly a voice called her name. Amba turned to see an old ascetic walking toward her. She gave a cry of welcome and delight and ran to throw herself at his feet, for this was none other than Hotravahana, her grandfather, who had given up his throne when his son came of age to rule, and who had gone to live with the other holy ones in the forest ashram.

Hotravahana helped Amba get to her feet and embraced her. As soon as she was in her grandfather's arms, Amba began to sob.

When her sobs began to quieten, Hotravahana said, "What is it, my child? What brings you here and in such distress? Tell me your sorrows."

Amba poured out all her pain and shame to her grandfather. She told him about the swayamvara and how Bhishma abducted her and her sisters, about Shalva's rejection, and about Bhishma's refusal to marry her.

Hotravahana listened to all of this patiently and compassionately.

When Amba's tale was done, he said, "Be comforted, my child. I know of one who may be able to reason with Bhishma. He will be coming to this ashram in a few days."

"Who is he, Grandfather?"

"He is a very great and holy man, but we must wait until he arrives before I say more."

The monks at the ashram welcomed Amba as their guest because her grandfather was there. As Hotravahana had said, a few days later, a holy man arrived at the ashram.

Hotravahana introduced Amba to him, saying, "Amba, this is Guru Bhargava. Bhargava, this is Amba, my granddaughter. She is troubled and seeks your aid. I think only you will be able to help her. Will you hear her tale?"

Bhargava said he would, and so Hotravahana told him all of Amba's sad story.

When the tale was done, Bhargava said to Amba, "Yes, Bhishma should marry you. I will ask him to. I am his guru, so he must obey me."

Bhargava had a messenger sent from the ashram to fetch Bhishma.

When Bhishma arrived, he greeted his guru with great joy and said, "Master, I am pleased to see you here. But why have you sent for me?"

Bhargava gestured toward Amba, who stood some distance away, watching the reunion of teacher and pupil.

Bhargava said, "Do you know that young woman?"

Bhishma recognized her, and an awful calm came over him. "Yes, I know her. She is the daughter of the king of Kasi. Fate has treated her very cruelly, and I am the cause of her distress. She wants me to marry her, but I cannot."

"Yes, you should marry her. It would be the right thing for you to do."

"I cannot. I swore a most solemn and holy oath that I would never marry and never sire children. I will not break my oath."

"Not even for your guru? That would be a most ungrateful thing for you to do."

"Alas, not even for my guru."

"A pupil who does not obey his guru is an abomination. But even so, I love you. Yet, you leave me no choice. I must either curse you or fight you. Which do you choose?"

"Master, we must fight."

"Very well. But we should not fight here, not on holy ground. Let us go somewhere else."

"There is a clearing not far from here. That is far enough away and open enough for a duel."

Forbidding anyone to follow them, Bhargava went with his pupil to the clearing Bhishma had told him about. Amba followed them secretly. She hid among the trees and watched the combat. As Amba looked on, master and pupil fought the most ferocious battle, each using their divine weapons against the other. Day and night, the battle raged on, and still neither could defeat the other. Finally, Bhishma felt he had no choice; he fit to his bowstring the divine weapon that would cause the end of the world.

Before Bhishma could let fly, the gods placed themselves in the space between Bhishma and Bhargava. Lord Shiva and Narada were at the fore, facing Bhishma. Shiva was tall and terrible and beautiful. His skin was ash-white, his throat blue, and his *jatas* flowed over his powerful shoulders.

Shiva said, "Hold, Devavrata! The world is not yours to destroy, nor has the time come for its destruction. Put down your bow."

Bhishma took a deep breath and did as Shiva bid him.

Shiva said, "The battle must stop. You are the pupil. It is your duty to withdraw."

Bhishma then went and knelt before his guru.

Bhargava raised Bhishma to his feet and said, "My Bhishma, you are well named, for indeed you are most terrible in battle. In all the world, there is no fighter greater than you, for even I could not defeat you."

Then Bhargava faced the place where Amba was hiding, for, by his holy wisdom, he knew that she was there.

The great guru said, "My child, I am sorry. Bhishma will not break his oath, and there is nothing I or anyone else can do about it. You must look elsewhere for a husband."

Amba let out a great choking sob and fled that place, weeping and stumbling, neither knowing nor caring whither she was bound.

Amba's Penance

Amba ran and ran through the forest, her clothing and hair torn by thorns, her feet bruised and blistered by tree roots and stones. Her weeping was of rage, not of sorrow, and in her soul was a burning desire to kill Bhishma, to exact revenge for what he had done to her.

Amba finally stopped running and sat down at the foot of a great tree and began to do penance. She refused herself food and water. She did nothing day in and day out but sit at the base of the tree and pray to Lord Shiva's son, the great Kartikeya. A long time passed, and one day Amba opened her eyes to see none other than Lord Kartikeya himself standing before her. She prostrated herself at his feet in worship.

"My child," Kartikeya said, "I have seen your penance, and I am pleased. I have also seen your desire that Bhishma should die. Behold, I give you this garland of lotus blossoms, whose blooms shall never wither. Whoever dons this garland will be the one to kill Bhishma."

Then Kartikeya gave Amba his blessing and vanished.

Amba knew what she needed to do. She went to all the kings in all the lands, one by one. She told them her story and how Lord Kartikeya himself had told her that the one who wore the garland would be able to kill Bhishma. One by one, every king and every Kshatriya she asked denied her request. Amba then went to King Drupada, the King of the Panchalas.

"My lord," she said, "you are my last hope. Every other king and Kshatriya has denied me. Take this garland. Kill Bhishma. You are the only one who can do it."

"My lady," Drupada said, "if you had asked me to fight anyone else, I would have gladly assented. But I will not fight Bhishma. I am not afraid to fight him. I simply will not. Bhishma is a righteous man, and it would be wrong for me to kill him, even assuming I could do so."

Amba stood speechless and enraged for a moment. Then she shrieked out her anger, threw the garland at one of the pillars in the hall, turned on her heel, and stormed away from Drupada's court, feeling that even the gods now wanted to cheat her. Drupada and the people of his court, for their part, were wary of the garland. Drupada gave orders that it was never to be touched, and so it hung there, unwithering, for a very long time.

Amba marched away from the land of the Panchalas. She left all human habitation behind and went to the places where the Rishis made their abodes. She walked across lonely wide plains and forded rivers. She climbed into the foothills, weaving her way through their forests. Then she began to climb the mountains, seeking only one mountain of them all, the holy Kailasa, where Lord Shiva makes his home. She finally collapsed in a snowdrift, unable to go any farther. A small cave was nearby. She entered it and began her penance once more, not eating, not drinking, not moving, praying night and day to Lord Shiva for his aid and protection.

A year went by, and when Amba finally opened her eyes, there before her stood Lord Shiva himself, handsome and white-skinned. Amba fell down before him and worshipped him.

Then Shiva said, "Be at peace, child. You will get all your desire. Bhishma shall die."

"By whose hand, Lord? Tell me, who will kill Bhishma?" Amba said.

"You will."

"But how can I—"

"Have no fear, Amba. You will not do this deed in this life but in your next."

"But when I am reborn, surely, I will remember nothing of this life. Then all my penance and prayers will have been for naught."

"By my grace, you shall be reborn immediately, with full knowledge of your past life."

For the first time in many years, Amba felt joy. "My lord, I cannot begin to thank you. Where will I be in the next life? Who will be my parents?"

"You will be the child of King Drupada. The lotus garland my son gave you is still there in Drupada's hall, hanging on a pillar, unwithered. It but waits for you to take it and fulfill your destiny."

Shiva then gave Amba his blessing and vanished.

Amba let out a joyous shout and then set about gathering wood, with which she made a great pyre. She threw herself into the roaring flames and so died.

Shikhandin

Now, King Drupada and his wife were childless and longed for a son.

They prayed to Lord Shiva and did penance, and finally, Shiva appeared to Drupada and said, "King Drupada, I have heard your prayers, and you shall be blessed with a child. The child shall be born a girl, but later in life, she will be transformed into a man."

"Lord Shiva," the king said, "I am grateful for your answer, but we don't need a daughter, even if she becomes a man later. May we please have a son? My throne needs an heir."

"I have given my gift to you as I think right. This is fate, and it cannot be changed." Then Shiva vanished.

As Shiva had promised, the queen was soon with child. When her time came, she gave birth to a healthy baby girl, but Drupada and his wife announced that the child was a boy named Shikhandin. Those who waited on the queen and attended her delivery were sworn to gravest secrecy never to reveal the true sex of the child. Drupada raised Shikhandin as a boy, teaching her the Vedas and the use of weapons and all the other things that a prince and a Kshatriya should know.

Shikhandin grew into a youth, tall and strong, but as yet, Shiva had not kept his promise that the girl would become a male in body as she was in training and spirit. Even so, the queen said that it was time Shikhandin was married, and thus a search for a suitable bride began. Drupada sought the hand of the daughter of Hiranyavarman, the King of the Dasharnakas. Hiranyavarman gladly agreed, and so the two young people were wed in a joyous celebration. But on the wedding night, it was discovered that Shikhandin was female in body, and both the bride and her father were greatly insulted. They went in great haste to Drupada's palace and demanded to see him.

"I agreed to marry my daughter to your son, not to your daughter!" Hiranyavarman shouted. "What trickery have you played on us? How dare you do such a thing! Be assured, I will bring my army and lay waste your lands and kill you and all your family and ministers to avenge this insult!"

"Please, my lord, wait," Drupada said. "We married Shikhandin to your daughter in good faith, for Lord Shiva himself told us that she would become a man in body one day. We thought that maybe this might happen at the wedding, but alas, it did not."

"Ah, so in addition to being a foul trickster, you are a liar now as well? All the more reason for me to invade sooner rather than later."

Then Hiranyavarman and his daughter left Drupada's court and went home to their country, where Hiranyavarman began to muster his army and prepare for war.

Drupada was distraught, for Hiranyavarman was a warrior like no other, and his army had never been defeated in battle.

"We are doomed for sure," he said to the queen. "Shiva has not kept his promise, and we shall soon be destroyed."

"Nay, my lord," the queen said. "Lord Shiva always keeps his word. We have but to pray."

And so she and Drupada began to pray to Shiva with all their might that calamity might be averted.

Knowing that she was the cause of all the strife and not wanting her parents killed, or the kingdom laid to waste, Shikhandin ran away into the forest. She came across a Yaksha who saw Shikhandin's distress and asked what was wrong. Shikhandin told the Yaksha about her disastrous marriage and Shiva's promise.

Then she said, "And now my family and my country are going to be destroyed all because of me. I didn't know what else to do but run away."

The Yaksha listened to Shikhandin's story and felt great compassion.

He said, "What if we were to exchange sexes? I shall give you my male sex, and I shall take on your female sex. Then you can go home and tell everyone that you are a man in body as well, and maybe King Hiranyavarman will be appeased. But I will only make you male for a short time. We must change back once you have saved your family and your country."

Shikhandin gratefully agreed to the Yaksha's plan, and when her body had been made male and the Yaksha's made female, she returned to her home, where she found all was in preparation for war.

"Mother! Father!" she cried. "Shiva's promise has come true! I am a man indeed!"

Shikhandin showed proof of what the Yaksha had done, and Drupada and his queen rejoiced. Perhaps they were saved after all, by the grace of Shiva and the kind Yaksha.

Drupada sent a messenger to Hiranyavarman, telling him that there had been a mistake and that Shikhandin was indeed a man. Hiranyavarman replied that he would believe that Shikhandin was male when his manhood had been properly tested. Drupada and Shikhandin agreed, so Hiranyavarman came to Drupada's palace with a group of the most beautiful women anyone had ever seen. One by one, they were sent into Shikhandin's apartments, and one by one, they came out very satisfied, saying that Shikhandin was indeed a man. Hiranyavarman and Drupada made peace on the spot, and Drupada commanded that a great banquet be held in honor of Hiranyavarman and in honor of Shikhandin's marriage.

When the banquet was over, Shikhandin stole out of the palace and went back to the forest to exchange sexes with the Yaksha as promised.

But when she arrived there, the Yaksha said, "I cannot change back with you, not ever. I am in service to Lord Kuvera, who says that I have shamed him and all Yakshas by my kindness to you. Therefore, I am to remain female, and you are to remain male."

Shikhandin felt pity for the Yaksha, but she also was elated for herself and for her family since she would not have to continue to delude her wife or parents-in-law and risk starting another war. She thanked the Yaksha for her sacrifice and went back home, grateful that Lord Shiva's promise had indeed come true.

And so it happened that many years later, Shikhandin was on the field of the great battle, fighting alongside the hero Arjuna, when Bhishma came into view. Both Arjuna and Shikhandin let fly with many arrows, all of which found their target. Bhishma touched the many arrows that pierced his body.

When he touched the one nearest his heart, he said, "This one is Amba's," and then he fell to the ground. Bhishma knew that this was his fate and that his life was at an end, so he released his spirit, which went to join his beloved mother Ganga in the heavens.

Ekalavya

This story takes place during the hero Arjuna's tutelage under the great Achaya (weapons master) Drona. Drona has promised Arjuna that he will become the greatest archer the world has ever known. Arjuna holds that promise close to his heart and works hard to make Drona's promise come true. However, a young Nishada lad named Ekalavya also has set his sights on becoming the world's greatest archer. But when he comes to Drona asking to become a student, Drona turns him away. Ekalavya is not a Kshatriya, but a Nishada, a member of a tribe of non-Indo-Aryan people who live in the forests, and so Drona cannot become his teacher. Undaunted, Ekalavya works by himself to become the greatest archer in the world.

A great warrior Arjuna might be, but he is a flawed human being. Here we see the depth of his pride and vanity, for when faced with Ekalavya's skill with the bow, Arjuna loses all heart. Only Ekalavya's willing sacrifice for Drona can restore Arjuna's self-respect. The wild boy from the forest thus shows that in many ways, he is nobler than the Kshatriya, who counts the god Indra as his spiritual father.

One evening, Drona was sitting in his garden enjoying the soft coolness of the air and the scent of the lotus blossoms. Seemingly from out of nowhere, a dark-skinned boy dressed in animal pelts ran up to Drona and fell at his feet.

"Master Drona," the boy said, "I wish to become one of your pupils. I wish to learn the art of archery."

"Who are you, young one?" Drona asked. "Where are you from, and who is your father?"

"My name is Ekalavya, Master. My father is Hiranyadhanush, King of the Nishadas of the forest."

"Ah, I see. Unfortunately, I cannot take you as my pupil. I can only take those who are Kshatriyas, and you are not of that rank." When Drona saw how disappointed the boy was, he added, "But you seem like a clever lad. I'm sure you'll find a way to learn archery all the same."

Ekalavya thanked Drona for his kindness and then returned to his forest home.

In the days that followed, Ekalavya collected clay from the riverbed and used it to make a statue of Drona. He searched his memory for every little detail that he could recall, and after much effort, he had created a clay model of Drona that was so accurate it almost seemed to be alive. Every day, Ekalavya knelt at the feet of his clay acharya, and every day, he practiced with his bow and arrows until he could hit any target he chose.

Years passed. Drona continued to teach his students and continued to turn out the finest warriors of any acharya in the world. One day, Arjuna and his classmates asked Drona whether they might have leave to go hunting.

"I suppose you may," Drona said. "You have all been working very hard and have earned some free time."

The students went into the forest with their bows and arrows and brought with them a keen-nosed hunting dog. The dog ran ahead of the hunting party, and soon he came to the place where Ekalavya was perched on a tree limb. The dog began to bark at Ekalavya, so the young Nishada began to shoot arrows at the animal. In no time at all, the dog's muzzle was sewn shut with seven arrows, a feat of amazing bowmanship. The dog went whining back to Arjuna and his friends, who all marveled at the skill of the unknown bowman—all but Arjuna, who burned with shame and envy.

Arjuna and the others went looking for the one who had shot their dog, and soon they found him in a forest clearing, practicing archery, while a clay statue of Drona looked on. None of the young Kshatriyas had ever seen an archer with such skill, which even Arjuna himself could not match.

Arjuna called out to the bowman, saying, "Who are you? What are you doing here?"

"I am Ekalavya, son of Hiranyadhanush, King of the Nishadas of the forest. I am practicing archery, for I am a pupil of the great Drona."

The hunting party went back to Drona's school to tend to their dog's wounds and tell their master about the wondrous bowmanship of the strange archer in the forest. Later that evening, when most of the students had gone to their chambers to rest, Arjuna sought out his master and found him sitting alone in his garden.

"Master Drona," Arjuna said, "my heart is very troubled by what happened in the forest today. You once told me that I was to be your finest pupil and the best archer in the world. But today, I saw bowmanship that puts my skills to shame, practiced by a no-account Nishada lad who says that you are also his teacher."

Drona had no answer for this at first, but then he remembered his encounter with Ekalavya some years before.

"Come with me," Drona said. "Let us pay your forest bowman a visit."

Arjuna led Drona to the place where he had met Ekalavya earlier that day. There they found the young man busy making arrows. When Ekalavya saw Drona, he rushed over to the old acharya and threw himself at his feet.

"Master Drona, welcome!" he said. "Have you come to see what progress I have made under your tutelage?"

"How can I be your master if you have lived here in the forest and I in my school?" Drona asked.

"Oh, quite easily. You have been here the whole time. Look!" Ekalavya pointed to the statue he had made.

"I see." Drona was impressed by the lifelike nature of the statue. "Well, if I am your master, and you are my pupil, then you must pay me my fee."

"Gladly, Master. Whatever you ask of me, I shall pay it."

"Give me your right thumb."

Ekalavya cheerfully severed his thumb and handed it to Drona. He bound up his wound, and then Drona showed him how to shoot with his remaining fingers. Ekalavya soon became a fearsome marksman, but he ever after lacked the skill and speed he had once had. And so it was that Drona's promise came true, and Arjuna became the best archer in the entire world.

The Burning of Khandava Forest

This excerpt from the Mahabharata *finds Arjuna and Krishna in conflict with Arjuna's spiritual father, the rain god Indra, who had enabled Arjuna's earthly parents to conceive him. The fire god Agni wishes Arjuna and Krishna's help in setting the Khandava Forest alight so that he may consume it with his flames. But since the forest is under Indra's protection, Agni will not be able to burn the forest without assistance.*

The destruction of the forest also inadvertently provides the seed that will grow into the great conflict between the Kaurava and Pandava princes that is at the heart of the Mahabharata*: the construction of the Pandava palace by an Ashura named Maya. The feud between the two clans begins when the Kandava prince Duryodhana mistakes a shiny floor in the Pandava palace for water and a still pond for a hard floor. Duryodhana is humiliated when he falls into the water. That insult, combined with Kaurava jealousy over the Pandavas' wealth, begins an escalating chain of confrontations that culminates in the apocalyptic battle at the climax of the epic.*

We also again see how the lines between good and evil are often blurred in Indian myth and philosophy. Maya is an Ashura and so technically can be classified as an evil being, but he is also sensitive, talented, and creative. When Maya flees the conflagration from which Agni commanded no creature must escape, he begs Arjuna and Krishna to spare his life. Arjuna sees that Maya is a worthy being and so lets him go, and in return, Maya agrees to construct a palace for the Pandavas. By saving Maya and asking him to build the palace, Arjuna thus launches the progress of the feud that Krishna foresees leading to carnage and destruction—a future Krishna accepts with equanimity since it is fated to happen.

Agni's Banquet

One fine day in the middle of summer, Krishna went to Arjuna and said, "It is too hot to stay here in the city. Let's go down to the Yamuna, near the Khandava Forest. We can eat on the banks of the river and swim in her waters, and maybe even take a walk in the shade of the forest. What say you?"

Arjuna agreed that this was a fine idea, so they invited their friends and their wives and asked servants to come along to prepare the meal and see to other things they might need. When everything was packed, and everyone had climbed into the carts that were to take them there, they set off for the river. Everyone was in a festive mood. They could not wait to bathe in the cool water and sit along the banks of the river. The happy party arrived at the river. The men went one way to bathe in the water, and the women went another. After everyone had had their fill of splashing and playing in the cool river, they came back to the bank and ate the fine meal that the servants had prepared.

Krishna especially was pleased to be there. He had grown up along the Yamuna, near another forest, and the river was part of his own history. When the meal was done, the sleepy men and women went to the tents that had been pitched by the servants to take a rest.

It was then that Krishna said to Arjuna, "Shall we go for a stroll in the forest?"

"Yes, let's do that," Arjuna replied.

The two friends walked companionably along the riverbank until they came to the eaves of the forest. They had hardly passed into the shadow of the trees when a holy man approached them. He had red-gold skin and golden hair, and his eyes were red.

Krishna and Arjuna both honored the holy man, who then said, "I am very hungry. Please give me something to eat."

"Certainly," Arjuna said. "If you continue along the riverbank behind us, you will come to our camp. Anyone there will be glad to give you as much food and drink as you wish."

"I do not wish that kind of food."

"What then can we give you?"

"The forest. I wish to eat this forest, all of it. I am Agni, the god of fire, and I have tried many times for many years to devour this forest, but within it lives Takshaka, the king of the serpents. Takshaka and Indra are great friends, and so every time I try to eat the forest, Indra sends rain. But I know both of you to be great warriors who know how to use divine weapons. Let me eat the forest. When it starts to rain, use your divine weapons to make it stop. Then I can eat until I am sated."

"Yes, we are masters of divine weapons, and we always have some about us, but we came here for a day of leisure along the river, not for a fight. We have no bows that can launch our divine arrows, nor do we have a chariot, and anyway, all we would have to pull a chariot are some sleepy carthorses whose fastest gait is a plod. But if you can get us the proper bows and chariots with fast horses, we can help you."

Agni agreed to get Krishna and Arjuna the things they needed. First, he went to Varuna, the god of the oceans, and asked to borrow Varuna's great bow, Gandiva, and a quiver of arrows that could never be emptied. He asked to borrow the chariot that belonged to Soma, the god of the moon, and some horses to pull it. Varuna and Soma gladly agreed, and they returned to the banks of the river with Agni to give the weapons and chariot to the two heroes. Varuna gave the beautiful bow and quiver of arrows to Arjuna, and Sma showed him to the chariot, which was pulled by four white horses who could run faster than the wind. Krishna offered to drive so that Arjuna could use his divine arrows to stop the rain. Varuna then gave to Krishna a great mace called Kaumodaki and a chakra disk called Sudarshana. Krishna and Arjuna were very pleased with their weapons and felt ready to take on Indra himself.

Arjuna said to Agni, "Begin your burning. We will hold back the rain."

Agni said, "I thank you. Please remember that I must consume everything within the forest to quell my hunger. And all of the creatures within the forest are evil, so let no living thing escape."

Then Agni turned himself into a great column of flame and began to burn the forest. First, he worked his way around its borders and then started moving toward the center. The flames and smoke rose up into the sky, reaching above the tops of even the highest trees. Krishna and Arjuna drove around and around the forest, faster than the wind, and all the while, Arjuna shot his divine arrows at anything that dared hop, run, or fly from out of the trees.

In his heavenly abode, Indra smelled the smoke from the burning and looked down to see the Khandava ablaze with fire. He saw Arjuna and Krishna driving around and around the forest, shooting down any living thing that tried to escape.

"How dare Agni burn my forest!" Indra cried. "He'll not get away with this."

Indra then summoned great storm clouds full of rain. He sent them to the forest and told them to rain on the trees until not one spark of the fire was left.

Agni saw the clouds coming. "Watch out!" he cried to Arjuna and Krishna. "Indra saw the forest ablaze, and now he's sending a big storm!"

Barely had Agni finished speaking when down came the rain. It rained as it had never rained before, great blinding sheets of water pouring out of the sky. But before the rain could put out the fire, Arjuna fired thousands of divine arrows into the sky. With the arrows, he made a great magical net that covered the forest like a dome, and when the net was complete, not a drop of water could get through.

Now, Indra's friend, the serpent king Takshaka, was not at his home in the forest when Agni started the fire, but his wife and children were. Takshaka's queen tried to fly out of the blaze, but Arjuna saw her and slew her with a single arrow. Takshaka's son, Ashwasena, also tried to fly out of the fire, but when Indra saw Arjuna readying his bow, he sent a great wind so strong that Arjuna could neither see nor move, and so Ashwasena was able to get away.

When the wind subsided, Arjuna shouted a challenge at Indra.

"That wind was a bold move, but you'll not stop us from letting Agni eat this forest," he said. "If you want a fight, come and fight with us! We'll see who is the stronger!"

With that, Arjuna sent a volley of arrows straight at his father.

Indra dodged the arrows and wielded his dread Vayavyastra, the weapon that sends winds like hurricanes. So strong did the winds blow that they began to blow out Agni's fires. Arjuna sent a wind weapon of his own against Indra's, and soon the tempest had died down, and Agni's fires blazed up once more.

The other gods who had been watching the battle became worried that Arjuna might defeat Indra, so they all grabbed their weapons and went down to fight too. Never has such a battle raged anywhere or at any time. The two noble heroes raced to and fro in their chariot, wielding their weapons here and there, and no matter how hard the gods tried to strike them, none could land a single blow. And although Indra was fighting Arjuna himself, he was very proud to see how great a warrior his son had become.

Just as Indra was poised to strike Arjuna with his mace, a voice from the heavens said, "Indra, stay your hand! Your friend Takshaka is not in the forest, and Ashwasena has escaped. The forest is fated to be consumed today. Do not fight with Arjuna and Krishna any longer. It is not right that a father fights his son this way, and Arjuna and Krishna can never be defeated."

Indra went down to the forest and stood before Arjuna and Krishna's chariot. The two heroes got out of the chariot and then put their palms together and bowed to Indra to do him honor.

"I have never seen such skill or such courage," Indra said. "Ask me for anything, and it shall be yours."

Krishna shook his head to say he wanted nothing from Indra.

But Arjuna fell at his father's feet and said, "O my father, please give me all the divine weapons you have."

When Indra heard Arjuna's request, he laughed for delight.

"Patience, my son! You will have all the divine weapons you will ever need. But I cannot give you all of mine until Lord Shiva gives you his own Pasupata. Then I will be able to turn all my divine weapons over to you, for this is your destiny." Then Indra said to Krishna, "Is there truly nothing you wish from me?"

Krishna said, "I only wish Arjuna to be my friend forever."

"Then so he shall be," Indra said, and with that, he gave the two brave Kshatriyas his blessing and returned to the heavens.

Arjuna and Maya

Now, when Agni was devouring the Khandava Forest, an Ashura named Maya was there. He had come to the forest to visit his friend Takshaka. Takshaka was not at home, and Maya had the misfortune of not leaving before Agni began to burn the forest. When the fire came roaring up, Maya fled as fast as he could to get away from the flames. Krishna saw Maya, a grand and ancient being, come running out of the forest with Agni in hot pursuit. Krishna made ready to throw his chakra to kill Maya.

Maya saw what Krishna was going to do, so he threw himself at Arjuna's feet and cried, "Please! Spare my life!"

Arjuna replied, "Have no fear. No one will kill you."

Krishna lowered his weapon, and Agni turned away since Maya was now under Arjuna's protection, and so Maya escaped the flames.

The forest burned on and on until nothing was left but ashes and smoldering tree stumps. Again, Agni appeared to Arjuna and Krishna, who put their palms together to honor him.

The fire god said, "Ah, that was the most magnificent repast. I have not feasted like that in the longest time. I thank you for your assistance, and in gratitude, I grant that you may go wherever you like in the world, whenever you like."

With that, Agni vanished.

Arjuna and Krishna walked along the riverbank toward their camp. On the way, they stopped to bathe in the cool water, and then they went to sit under a tree to rest. When they were ready, they got up and resumed walking back to their camp. They hadn't gone far when Maya came to them. He put his palms together and bowed to Arjuna.

Then he said, "O mighty Kshatriya, you saved me from Agni's wrath. I wish to know what I might do for you in return."

"I wish nothing for myself," Arjuna replied. "For me, the deed is enough. I never expect anything in return from those I help."

"But I wish to show my gratitude. Will you allow me that? It won't be repayment, just something to make you happy, which would also please me very much. I am an architect, the greatest in the world. I have built palaces and pleasure gardens, the likes of which the world has never seen. I have laid out entire cities, planned their streets and buildings, placed fountains and gardens within them. Let me build something for you."

"I do not wish to offend you, and I know of your skill, but I cannot accept that gift." Arjuna saw that Maya was terribly crestfallen, so he added, "Perhaps you might do something for Krishna instead, and I will accept it as also having been done for me. When Krishna is pleased, I also am pleased."

"Very well. Please tell me what I might do for you, O noble Krishna."

Krishna thought for a moment. Then he said, "I would like you to build a palace for Prince Yudhisthira of the Panadavas. Make it the most beautiful building you have ever made."

Maya was overjoyed to be given such a task. He immediately drew up plans for the palace, and when Krishna and Arjuna had returned home, they introduced Maya to Yudhisthira and showed him the plans. Yudhisthira was greatly pleased and honored and bade Maya begin the work as soon as he was able.

Maya said, "I ask leave to depart for a little while. In my abode, I have a great quantity of diamonds and other gems that I would like to use in decorating the palace. May I have some men to help me carry everything? There is a great quantity." Then Maya said to Arjuna, "I also have there a great club that perhaps your brother Bhima would like to have, and a conch shell called Devadatta that I would like to give to you, Arjuna, if you will allow it."

Arjuna agreed to take the shell with gratitude.

Maya went back to his home at the bottom of lake in the mountains near the abode of Shiva. He collected up all the multitude of gems and other precious things, as well as the club for Bhima and the conch he had promised Arjuna, and returned to Indraspratha. There he made a grand palace for Yudhisthira, which had a high dome that gleamed in the sun. Every wall was covered with something precious, be it gems or tapestry, or paintings. In the center was a limpid pool that was home to golden fish and turtles. The steps leading to the pool were made of crystal, and the floor and pillars surrounding it were of the finest marble. So still and clear were the waters of the pool that the unwary might think them made of crystal like the stairs and so fall in when they tried to walk on them.

Maya did not forget to create many gardens for the palace. The gardens were planted with all manner of trees and flowers, and they also had pools in which grew the sweet lotus. Anyone who smelled the scent of those gardens thought they surely had been transported to paradise.

For fourteen months, Maya worked on Yudhisthira's palace. When it was complete, Maya showed Arjuna and Yudhisthira all around it, and Yudhisthira was grateful and awed.

Then Maya said to Arjuna, "See? I have completed the work that Krishna set for me. I hope it pleases you."

"It does indeed please me," Arjuna said.

"I must go now. But before I leave, I tell you this: You have a celestial chariot drawn by celestial steeds, and the noble ensign of Hanuman the monkey god is on your standard. From henceforth you shall be known as Swetavahana, He of the White Horses, and as Kapidhvaja, He of the Monkey Standard. I wish you all joy and many victories."

Then Maya and Arjuna embraced.

Maya returned home, laden with many rich gifts from Yudhisthira.

Bhima and Hanuman

Bhima is another of the great heroes of the Mahabharata. *He is Arjuna's brother—since the two share the same human parents. But whereas Arjuna's spiritual father is the storm god Indra, Bhima's spiritual father is Vayu, god of the winds. Bhima and his brothers are all married to Draupadi, a Pandava princess, but Bhima also has a son, Ghatokacha, by his other wife, the demoness Hidimbi. Ghatokacha's half-demon origin gives him special magic powers, such as flight.*

Bhima's special gift is his prodigious strength. This he received when he was given a healing potion by Nagas (divine half-human, half-serpent beings), who rescued a young Bhima after he was poisoned and thrown into a river by his cousin, Duryodhana, and Duryodhana's uncle Shakuni. The Nagas' potion also made Bhima immune to all poisons and venoms.

In this story, we join Bhima and his Pandava companions while they are lodging in a mountain ashram and waiting for Arjuna to return from a journey. The Pandavas are staying at the ashram because they were exiled when Yudhisthira was cheated out of his kingdom and wealth in a rigged game of dice with the dastardly Kaurava prince Duryodhana. Here we learn that while Bhima's wits may not match his strength, he loves his wife dearly and would do anything for her. We also learn that Bhima is very devoted to the monkey-god Hanuman, with whom Bhima shares a common father. He will happily talk about Hanuman's exploits to anyone who sits still long enough, including a disguised Hanuman himself.

The mountain ashram where the Pandavas had taken shelter was in a beautiful part of the world. There were many flowering shrubs and trees in the forests, the air was continually perfumed by cedars, and the waters ran crystal-clear from the peaks above. Bhima's wife Draupadi loved to go for walks under the shade of the trees, and often her husband would accompany her.

One day as Bhima and Draupadi were strolling through the forest, they caught the scent of a wild and intoxicating perfume.

"Oh, I must see where this scent is coming from," Draupadi said.

Bhima agreed, and so they followed the scent until suddenly a breeze blew up and deposited a flower at Draupadi's feet. Draupadi picked it up, sniffed its perfume, and then passed the flower to Bhima.

"This is the source of that scent," Draupadi cried. "Oh, smell it, husband. It's like the perfume of paradise itself!"

Bhima took the flower and inhaled its scent. Draupadi was right; this was no ordinary flower. Bhima felt like its scent was moving through his entire body, a sensation he had never felt before, and that was like no other.

"Let's take this back to the ashram and put it in some water," Draupadi said, "and perhaps tomorrow you can come back to the forest and see whether you can find more flowers like this. I want to give this one to Yudhisthira, but I'd like more for myself. I desire to be surrounded by this scent for as long as possible."

"I will gladly look for more of these flowers for you, my wife," Bhima said. "But for now, we should return to the ashram. It is nearly sunset."

Bhima and Draupadi returned to the ashram, where Draupadi gave the flower to Yudhisthira. All the Pandavas exclaimed at the beauty of the flower's scent and were delighted to hear that Bhima intended to find more such blossoms in the morning.

At sunrise, Bhima took his weapons and his conch shell and set out for the forest. He strode mightily through the thick trees, and the noise of his powerful footsteps was such that even the lions and elephants fled in fear. On he strode, climbing effortlessly up the mountainside, putting up flocks of birds and making tigers and bears run back into their dens. He came to a forest of plantain trees and decided to make a path for himself by uprooting the trees and tossing them aside. This made even more noise than his footsteps did, and the animals and birds all trembled, thinking that the end of the world was at hand.

Bhima raged his way through the forest until he came to a lake dotted with fragrant lotus, where he put down his weapons and went for a swim. He felt so refreshed afterward that he blew a blast on his conch shell. When the lions and wolves and birds heard that blast, they all began screeching and howling and growling and roaring with fear.

Now, Hanuman, the monkey god, was also in the forest, not far from the lake. He heard Bhima's striding steps and the sound of the trees as they were uprooted and thrown aside. He heard the blast of Bhima's conch, and he heard the terror of the animals and birds.

"I must do something about this Bhima," Hanuman said. "I do love him so, but he is upsetting all the creatures who live in the forest, and if he's not careful, he's going to get himself into trouble he can't get out of."

Hanuman, therefore, turned himself into an aged monkey. In that form, he went and laid himself across the trail that Bhima was taking. Bhima came striding along and saw the aged creature lying in his path. Bhima didn't want to harm the monkey, but neither did he want to step over it, and there was no room on either side of the trail for him to pass, so he roared a lion's roar at the monkey as loud as he could.

The monkey didn't flinch at all at Bhima's roar.

He merely opened his eyes, turned to look at Bhima, and said, "Why must you make such a racket? Can't you see that I'm trying to take a nap? Also, it's not very polite for one who knows Dharma to try to frighten simple animals. For shame. If you know anything at all about Dharma, you should know that. Besides, this forest is no place for you. If you have any sense at all, you'll turn around and go back where you came from. If you like, you can sit here with me and eat some fruit first, but only after you've told me who you are."

Bhima, at first, was astonished to hear a monkey speaking like a human would.

Then he answered, "My name is Bhima, son of Kunti and of Vayu, the god of the winds. Now that you know who I am, you can return the favor by telling me who you are."

"Oh, I am nothing but a simple monkey who lives here in the forest. There. Now you know who I am, and if you're not going to eat fruit with me, you need to turn around and go home."

"That I'll not do. Move aside."

The monkey sighed an aged sigh. "I simply can't. I'm so tired. I don't have the energy to do anything at all, and here you are, a great, strong Kshatriya, wandering through my forest without so much as a by-your-leave, bellowing at everyone like some great bull elephant and knocking over trees that have never done you any harm. If you're so energetic, maybe you should just jump over me."

"I'd rather not do that, either. It wouldn't be polite since you are so much older than I am. But I need to continue my journey, and I'll jump over you just like Hanuman leaped over the ocean if that's what I have to do, whether it's polite to do that or not."

"Hanuman? Who on earth is this Hanuman person, and how can anyone jump over the whole ocean? I think you're making things up, and it's not polite to tell false tales to your elders, either."

Bhima blinked in astonishment. "You . . . you honestly don't know who Hanuman is? You're a monkey yourself, and you don't know who Hanuman is? I think maybe you're the one who's making up stories now, and I feel a great deal easier in my mind about having to jump over you now that I've heard you don't know who Hanuman is."

"Well, it certainly sounds like something has been lacking in my education. How about you tell me all about Hanuman? Tell me the story about how he jumped over the ocean. That sounds interesting, and maybe a nice story will help me get back to sleep."

"Very well. The first thing you need to know is that Hanuman is my brother. His father, Vayu, is also my father, as I already told you."

"Go on. And don't leave anything out."

"Right. One day, Sita, the wife of the great hero Rama—you do know who Rama is, don't you?"

"Yes, I believe I have heard something about him. Continue your tale."

"Well, one day, Ravana, the evil King of Lanka, kidnapped Sita and brought her to his island fortress. Hanuman and Rama looked high and low and up and down for her until finally, Hanuman found out where she was. There was no time to waste, so he simply leaped from the shore, flew over the ocean, and landed at Ravana's fortress. He and Rama had many dangers to face before they finally rescued Sita, but that whole battle began with Hanuman's great leap."

"That was quite a tale," Hanuman said.

"Yes, and you should know that since Hanuman is my brother, I'm just as strong as he is, so you need to either move aside or be moved by me."

"Oh, dear. You certainly are a fellow of a single idea. It's a shame I'm feeling so poorly. Maybe you don't need to move all of me. Just shift my tail, will you? That will make enough room for you to walk around me on the path."

Bhima stifled a chuckle. He thought to himself that he would not only move the monkey's tail but use it to pick up the monkey and fling him bodily out of the way.

What he said out loud was, "Certainly, old one. I'll just move your tail, and then we'll both be satisfied."

Bhima stepped over to where the monkey's tail was draped across the path. He reached down with one powerful hand to pick it up but found that it wouldn't budge. Bhima grasped the tail with both hands and tried to lift it, but he couldn't even get it off the ground. He pulled and heaved and strained until his body was dripping with sweat, and his great muscles were bulging, and the veins were standing out on his body, but nothing he could do would move the monkey's tail. Finally. he gave up. He took a chastened step back and put his palms together to honor the monkey.

Bhima said, "You are no simple monkey who lives in the forest. You are something much more. I apologize for my rudeness. I should have been more polite to you, and that was my duty even if I had been able to move your tail. Please tell me who you truly are."

"I accept your apology," Hanuman said. "And I am Hanuman himself, the son of Vayu and companion of Rama. I am your brother. Rama and Sita gave me this forest to live in. I stopped you from going any farther along this path because it is forbidden to mortals. Only the gods can use this trail, and besides, the flowers you are looking for are in a different part of the forest."

Bhima fell down before Hanuman. "Oh, this day, I am truly blessed. Today I have seen my brother, the son of Vayu! Grant me one thing, O elder brother. Let me see you as you appeared the day you leaped the ocean. That tale is close to my heart, and I would see you in your glory."

"I would show you if I could, younger brother, but alas, I cannot. That time has passed and will not come again. This is the form I have now, and it is the only form that you are allowed to see."

Then Hanuman imparted much wisdom to Bhima, about the world and everything in it, and about the Dharma.

When Hanuman was done with his telling, Bhima said, "Please, please show me the form you were in when you leaped the ocean. It is a true desire of my heart that I should see you thus."

Hanuman considered it again for a moment. "Very well."

He closed his eyes and began to grow in size. He grew and grew and grew until he towered over the treetops, and as he grew, his body glowed brighter and brighter until it shone like the sun, and Bhima could no longer look at it.

Again, Bhima put his palms together in honor of Hanuman and said, "Lord Hanuman, truly you are glorious! What a battle it must have been—the day you and Rama went to Lanka to fight with Ravana to rescue the fair Sita. But now you are too bright and too terrible for me to look at. Please diminish your form so that we can speak together some more."

"Yes, I fought bravely against Ravana, but it was Rama who killed the bastard, and it was right that I let him do so. Now, you have your own brothers' welfare to carry, just as I carried the brave Rama's, so you need to go back to them.

"But first, I will tell you how to find the flowers your beloved wife cherishes. Go along this path to the Saugandhika Forest. In that forest is a garden that belongs to Kubera. The garden is guarded by Yakshas and Rakshasas. Do not take those flowers rashly. Remember that humans must respect the gods with prayers, worship, and sacrifices. Always remember to follow the Dharma, and that your duty as a Kshatriya is to protect others."

Then Hanuman shrank in size, and when he was no bigger than Bhima, he took his half-brother into a warm embrace. Bhima felt great strength flowing through his body, and he wept with the joy of his brother's embrace.

Hanuman also had tears in his eyes. "Brave Bhima, little brother, you need to go back to your wife and your companions. Please do not tell them what passed between us in this forest. It would not be right for people to come here seeking me out. You must leave now. Divine beings are on their way, and you must not be here when they arrive.

"Before you leave, however, ask me a boon. Anything you ask, you shall have. Would you like me to capture Duryodhana and destroy the city of the Kauravas? I will gladly do that for you. I will bring your enemy here for you to deal with as you please."

Bhima replied, "It is enough that you wish me well. If you wish me well, I know that my brothers and I will be victorious."

"Then it is done. I wish you and your brothers well. I will ride on Arjuna's standard, and anyone who sees it will flee in fear. Now, follow the path I have shown you. You must leave, and I must stay."

Hanuman then vanished, leaving Bhima alone on the forest path.

Bhima gazed for a moment at the sacred spot where Hanuman had stood, and then he resumed his journey. He went through thick forest and up steep hillsides, journeying ever onward until he came to the eaves of the Saugandhika Forest. He plunged into the forest and strode on until he came to a lake at the foot of Mount Kailasa. The lake had the clearest water Bhima had ever seen, dotted with sweet lotuses. Here were the flowers that his beloved Draupadi asked for!

Bhima had arrived at the garden of Kubera, god of wealth. All the waters and flowers here were under his protection and guarded by fierce Yakshas and Rakshasas. When Bhima stepped toward the lake, he suddenly found himself surrounded by dozens of fierce beings, all of them armed and spoiling for a fight.

"What are you doing here?" their leader demanded. "Don't you know that this is Kubera's private garden? Mortals aren't welcome. Go home before we kill you."

Bhima replied, "Greetings to you. My name is Bhima. I am the younger brother of Prince Yudisthira. He and I and our companions are staying at an ashram not far from here. I came to this garden because one of its flowers drifted onto the path where I was walking with my beloved Draupadi. Draupadi asked me to get her more of the flowers, and so I am here to get them because I wish to please her."

"That is a noble quest for a loving husband," the leader of the Rakshasas said, "but even so, you are not welcome here. You cannot drink from the lake or take any of the flowers without Kubera's leave. Even the gods and other divine beings have to ask him first."

"If it is Kubera's garden, then where is he? I don't see him anywhere. This is just a lake in the mountains. It belongs to me and to everyone else, just the same as it belongs to Kubera. Also, I will not beg, not of Kubera nor of anyone else. I am Kshatriya, and it is against Dharma for me to beg from anyone, even if that one is a god himself."

With that, Bhima made a great leap. He jumped past the army of Yakshas and Rakshasas and straight into the waters of the lake. The Rakshasas roared and charged at Bhima, who whirled to face them, wielding his great mace. The Rakshasas and Yakshas attacked and attacked, but they were no match for Bhima's skill or strength. Soon, Bhima had killed many of them and put the rest to flight. The battle over, Bhima plunged into the waters of the lake. He swam about collecting lotuses to take back to his beloved Draupadi, sometimes taking a drink of the clear water, which was the most refreshing thing he had ever tasted.

Meanwhile, the surviving guardians of the lake rushed back to Kubera's palace.

They went before Kubera and said, "Lord Kubera, there is an intruder in your lake! It is Bhima. We told him he had to ask your leave to go into the water and take flowers, but he wouldn't listen. We tried to guard the lake, but he fought with us and defeated us. What are we to do now?"

Kubera smiled. "You did your duty well, do not fear. Let brave Bhima drink his fill and take as many flowers as he likes to give to his wife."

Now, while Bhima was fighting with the guardians of the lake, a great wind began to blow, and the sky was darkened with many clouds. Yudhisthira and Draupadi saw this and wondered what was happening.

"Has Bhima returned yet?" Yudhisthira asked.

"No, he hasn't," Draupadi replied, "and the wind and darkening sky are worrying. I wish I knew that he was safe."

"I'll ask his son Ghatokacha to take us to the Saugandhika. If Bhima needs help, Ghatokacha and I should be there to aid him."

"Please take me with you. It was I who asked him to get the flowers, and I'll never forgive myself if he has been harmed in doing that task for me."

Draupadi and Yudhisthira went to Ghatokacha and asked him to fly them to the forest where Bhima was. Ghatokacha readily agreed. Tucking Draupadi under one arm and Yudhisthira under the other, he flew as swiftly as he could to Kubera's lake. When the three companions arrived, they saw the lakeshore littered with the bodies of all the beings Bhima had slain and Bhima himself wading out of the lake with his arms full of lotus blossoms.

Draupadi ran to embrace her husband with a cry, saying, "Oh, Bhima! We were afraid something bad had happened to you. Are you well?"

"Yes, my wife, I am well. I had to fight many enemies, as you can see, but I found your flowers and have many of them here for you," Bhima replied.

Just then, Kubera appeared. "Welcome, friends. I see you have come to join brave Bhima, who is already a guest here in my garden. Won't you join us for a while?"

"We would be honored," Yudhisthira said, "but we were waiting for Arjuna at the ashram. We should go back there so that we do not miss him when he returns."

"Arjuna will not be returning for some time. Please stay with me for a week and then go back to the ashram. That way, I shall have the pleasure of your company for a time, and you will be back at the ashram when your friend arrives."

Yudhisthira and the others accepted Kubera's invitation with gratitude. Ghatokacha flew back to the ashram to get the other Pandavas staying there. They all spent a delightful week as Kubera's guests before returning to the ashram to await Arjuna.

Here's another book by Matt Clayton that you might like

Free Bonus from Captivating History (Available for a Limited time)

Hi History Lovers!

Now you have a chance to join our exclusive history list so you can get your first history ebook for free as well as discounts and a potential to get more history books for free! Simply visit the link below to join.

Captivatinghistory.com/ebook

Also, make sure to follow us on Facebook, Twitter and Youtube by searching for Captivating History.

Bibliography

The Bhagavata Purana. Delhi: Motilal Banarsidass Publishers, [1950]1999.

Aiyar, B. V. Kamesvara. *The Purusha Sukta.* Madras: G. A. Natesan & Co., 1898.

Chakraburtty, Sneh. *The Origin of Meditation.* Delhi: New Age Books, 2009.

Dharma, Krishna. *Mahabharata: The Greatest Spiritual Epic of All Time.* Badger, CA: Torchlight Publishing, 1999.

Ganguli, Kisari Mohan. *The Mahabharata of Krishna-Dwaipayana Vyasa (18 Volumes).* Calcutta: Bharata Press, [1889] 2014.

Griffith, Ralph T. H. *The Hymns of the Rig Veda, Translated with a Popular Commentary, Vol. 2.* Benares: E. J. Lazarus and Co., 1897.

Husain, Shahrukh. *Demons, Gods & Holy Men from Indian Myths & Legends.* New York: Schocken Books, 1987., and Bee Willey. *Indian Myths.* London: Evans Brothers Ltd., 2005.

Lal, P. *The Mahabharata of Vyasa, Book One: The Complete Adi Parva.* 2nd ed. Calcutta: Writers Workshop, 2013., *The Mahabharata of Vyasa, Book Two: The Complete Sabha Parva.* Calcutta: Writers

Workshop, 2005., *The Mahabharata of Vyasa, Book Three: The Complete Vana Parva*. Calcutta: Writers Workshop, 2005.

Mackenzie, Donald A. *Indian Myth and Legend*. London: The Gresham Publishing Company, Ltd., 1913.

Menon, Ramesh. *Bhagavata Purana*. 2 vols. New Delhi: Rupa Publications India Pvt. Ltd., 2007., *The Mahabharata: A Modern Rendering (2 Volumes)*. New York: iUniverse, Inc., 2006.

Pattanaik, Devdutt. *Jaya: An Illustrated Retelling of the Mahabharata*. n.p.: Penguin Books, 2010.

Phillips, Charles, Michael Kerrigan, and David Gould. *The Eternal Cycle: Indian Myth*. London: Duncan Baird Publishers, 1998.

Rao, Shanta Rameshwar. *The Mahabharata*. Hyderabad: Orient Longman Pvt. Ltd., [1968] 2002.

Satyamurti, Carole. *Mahabharata: A Modern Retelling*. New York: W. W. Norton & Company, 2015.

Subramaniam, Kamala. *Srimad Bhagavatam*. 14th ed. Mumbai: Bharatiya Vidya Bhavan, 2015., *Mahabharata*. Bombay: Bharatiya Vidya Bhavan, 1977.

Wilson, H. H. *The Rig-Veda-Sanhitá: A Collection of Ancient Hindu Hymns, Vol. 6*. London: Trübner and Co., [1850]1888.

www.ingramcontent.com/pod-product-compliance
Lightning Source LLC
Chambersburg PA
CBHW050512240426
43673CB00004B/199